CW01151441

Sake with Desserts

Makiko Tejima

Osakeとスイーツの世界へようこそ！

〈日本酒とスイーツ〉、この組み合わせを聞いて、「おいしそう」と思う人はあまりいないでしょう。塩を少しずつなめながら酒を飲むというのが、古くからの習慣であったことからも分かるように、日本酒は、塩気のあるものとよく合うというのが定説です。けれど、お正月にお節料理をつまみながら日本酒を飲んでいるときなど、黒豆やきんとんと意外な相性を示すことがあり、もしかしたら甘いものともいけるのかもしれないと思うようになりました。

2001年に、イタリアのスローフード協会が主催するチーズ祭りに招かれ、日本酒を紹介する機会に恵まれました。味も香りも日本ではまず口にすることがないようなヨーロッパ各地のチーズと、色々なタイプの日本酒を食べ合わせてみて、日本酒の懐の深さを再認識しました。なかでも印象的だったのは、ジャムをのせて、デザート感覚で食べるチーズと日本酒が素晴らしいマリアージュ（フランス語で結婚の意味）を示してくれたことです。この経験が、私に日本酒とスイーツの世界への扉を開いてくれました。

伝統的なものを新しい視点で、普段の暮らしのなかに取り入れて楽しむことをコンセプトに、日本酒をOsakeと表現し、テーブルコーディネートと共に30種類の組み合わせを提案しています。味の組み合わせだけでなく、どんな器で飲んだり、食べたりするかという食文化も、伝統という歴史のなかで、日々変化していることです。「食卓を囲む」という、日々当たり前に繰り返されることのなかにこそ、伝統を継承するための、たくさんの新しい試みの機会があると信じています。そんな新しい試みのひとつとして、未知なる〈Osakeとスイーツ〉の世界を、存分にお楽しみください。

Welcome to the World of O-sake* with Desserts!

〈O-sake with Desserts〉 This combination may not sound complementary to many people, since it is generally believed that o-sake goes best with salty dishes.

However, when I ate traditional New Year dishes, such as sugary black beans, I felt that o-sake might be compatible with desserts.

In 2001, I took part in a cheese festival held by the Italian Slow Food Association in Italy. I introduced o-sake at that event. It was then that I realized that o-sake really did go very well with European cheeses. Most impressively, I found that dessert cheeses with jam made a perfect marriage to o-sake. For me, this opened the door to the combination of o-sake with desserts.

In this book, thirty combinations of o-sake and desserts are presented, along with appropriate table settings. I believe that we can try new ideas, in a traditional framework and food culture, even when it comes to daily meals.

Please enter into the world of o-sake with desserts with me. Kampai!

* In Japanese, "o" is an honorific prefix.

食卓の雰囲気を演出する6つの気分

　Osakeとひとことでいっても、たくさんの種類があって、何を基準に選んでいいかわからない、という声をよく聞きます。ましてや、〈Osakeとスイーツ〉の組み合わせともなれば、なおさらです。そこでこの本では、普段の暮らしのなかで〈Osakeとスイーツ〉を楽しむ5つのシーン、アペリティフ、ブランチ、パーティー、アフタヌーン、ディジェスティフを設定しました。さらに、そのシーンごとに、〈6つの気分〉からOsakeとスイーツの組み合わせ、コーディネートを選べるようになっています。

　食卓の雰囲気は、いつ、どこで、誰と一緒かなど、その時々の状況によって大きく変わりますが、食卓を囲む人、ひとりひとりの気分にも大きく左右されるものです。ゆっくり落ち着いて楽しみたいと思っている人と、派手に騒いで楽しみたいと思っている人が同じ食卓を囲んでも、心地よい食卓の雰囲気をつくることはできません。ですから、こんな気分で楽しんでもらいたいというメッセージを、食卓で使うテーブルウエアの色、形、素材などに込め、雰囲気を演出することが大切です。

　この本に登場する「アフロディジアック」「インヴィゴラティング」「セダティブ」「スティムラント」「ユーホリック」「レギュラティング」という〈6つの気分〉は、英国における、アロマテラピーの第一人者のひとりである、ロバート・ティスランド氏が、アロマテラピーに使用するエッセンシャルオイルを分析したものを参考に、その気分を色彩心理学的視点から独自にカラー分類したものです。

　私が主宰する Kitchen & Dining スクール彩食絢美では、このカラー分類に基いた6つのスタイルによって、テーブルコーディネートの専門技術を身に付けるという指導法を、12年余り実践し、多くの卒業生たちを世に送り出しています。

●参考文献／ロバート・ティスランド「サイコ・アロマテラピー」
©Tisserand Aromatherapy Ltd.

Please see page 007 for the English translation.

Aphrodisiac
Regulating　　Invigorating
Euphoric　　Sedative
Stimulant

〈Osakeとスイーツ〉を楽しむにあたって、是非この〈気分の演出〉も参考にしてみてください。きょうはこんな気分だけど、どんな〈Osakeとスイーツ〉がいいのか、気分を変えたいのだけれど、どんな〈Osakeとスイーツ〉を選ぼうか、などというように、右ページに示す気分を表すイメージカラーのインデックスからページを開いてみてください。思いがけない〈おいしさ〉に、きっと出合えるはずです。

To best enjoy o-sake and dessert, consult the color indexes and choose the stagecraft suitable for your mood. I am sure that you will be pleasantly surprised.

アフロディジアック
ギリシャ神話のなかの、愛と美の女神、アフロダイテを語源にもつこのことばには、媚薬、催淫剤の意味があります。おとなの女性として、成熟した魅力をアピールしたい気分のときに。

Aphrodisiac
The word aphrodisiac derives from Aphrodite, the Greek goddess of love and beauty. This mood is suitable when you would like to appeal to your sensuality as a mature woman.

インヴィゴラティング
元気づけるという意味のこのことばどおり、落ち込んでいて気分がさえない、やる気がしないというときに、楽しく、さわやかな気分にしてくれます。

Invigorating
When you feel languid or depressed, this combination will cheer you up.

セダティブ
静める、鎮静剤という意味をもつこのことばから、普段着の自分にもどって、落ち着いた気持ちを取りもどしたい、自然に親しみたい、そんな気分のときにぴったりです。

Sedative
This coordination is effective when you would like to cool down and relax, or commune with nature.

スティムラント
刺激性の、興奮剤ということばの意味から、欧米人から見た東洋的エキゾチズムを表現しました。いつもとはちょっと違う気分で楽しみたいときに。

Stimulant
To feel stimulated or to experience something a little out of ordinary, how about experiencing Oriental exoticism? Try this when you feel like having a change.

ユーホリック
女性ならば誰もが夢見る、ロマンティックな甘い世界。ユーフォリア（幸福感）に通じる、やさしく満たされた気分です。

Euphoric
This mood is what women dream of, a romantic world, filled with sweet feelings.

レギュラティング
規則正しくする、調整するということばの意味から、シンプルでスタイリッシュな気分を演出しました。日常の煩雑さを忘れ、静かに、そしてクリエイティブに楽しみたい気分のときに。

Regulating
Here, we produced simple and stylish coordinations. To return to your natural self, or to feel more creative, please try these.

「私のOsake」に出合うために

　Osakeを選ぶとき、何を手がかりに選びますか？　原料米や精米歩合をもとに選ぶ人は、相当なOsake上級者です。私など日頃は、ラベルデザインやネーミングに頼って選ぶことがよくあります。でも、自分好みのOsakeに出合うこと、この難しそうな課題を解くカギは、実はとてもシンプルなことなのです。

　「この世の中には、たったふたつの味しかないんだよ。おいしいか、おいしくないか」。パリ在住の、ある著名なフランス人ソムリエが、当時ワインの味について勉強中であった私に、最後のレッスンで教えてくれたことです。おいしいか、おいしくないか、これは個人的な好みの問題で、いきつくところ、味というのは嗜好の問題につきるということです。

　日本全国では、2000近い蔵元が日本酒を製造しており、その数はおよそ1万銘柄にもおよぶと言われています。それほどの数のなかから、自分がおいしい！と思えるOsakeに出合えたら、それはもう素敵な恋人に巡り合ったと同じくらい幸せなことだと思うのです。そのためには、まず、自分の目で確かめ、味わってみる以外に方法はありません。専門家のアドバイスは、確かに有益な情報が多いのですが、それだけに頼っていては、「私の恋人」と呼べる、「私のOsake」には決して出合えません。とはいっても、すべての銘柄を飲んでみるには、人生は短すぎます。そこで、まずは味の指標として、甘口か、辛口か、を基準に飲んでいくことをおすすめします。

　甘辛は、味覚の原点ともいえる感覚です。造り手が発信する、この甘辛のタイプを指標に、一度に2、3種類の違うOsakeを飲んでみてください。味というのは、相対的に比較していくことで、違いがとても理解しやすくなります。同じ甘口でも、私はこちらのほうがおいしく感じるなど、そんなとろから「私のOsake」探しは始まります。素敵な出合いに恵まれるように、まずはLet's try!

Please see page 007 for the English translation.

日本酒造組合中央会が、飲み手の立場から
調査研究を続けている、甘辛表示に基く分類です。

清酒の甘辛表示
■甘辛推定式：Y＝S－A＋2
　S：清酒中のグルコース含量（g／100ml）
　A：清酒の酸度
　（上記S、Aの分析は国税庁所定分析法による）
■甘辛表示は、上記推定式の数値により次の
　4段階とする。
　甘口：3.9以上、やや甘口：3.1〜3.8、
　やや辛口：2.3〜3.0、辛口2.2以下

■ The classification described below is formulated by the Japan Sake Brewers Association.

■ Sweetness／Dryness Formula: Y＝S－A＋2
S: The amount of glucose in sake（g／100ml）
A: The acidity of sake.
(The analyses of the aforementioned S and A are conducted in accordance with the method prescribed by the National Tax Administration Agency of Japan.)

■ The type of taste is classified according to the following four classifications based on the formula.
Sweet: 3.9 or higher
Slightly sweet: Between 3.1 and 3.8
Slightly dry: Between 2.3 and 3.0
Dry: 2.2 or less

甘口 Sweet	やや甘口 Slightly sweet	やや辛口 Slightly dry	辛口 Dry	発泡酒 Sparkling sake	古酒 Aged sake

※左記、甘辛4分類にこの本独自のマークを付け、
　P.013〜P.087の各ページに表示しています。
※この他、発泡酒と古酒もアイコンで表示しました。
※ These icons indicate four types of taste,
　sparkling sake, and aged sake, respectively.

Six Moods for Enjoying O-sake（P.004）

Some say it is difficult to make a nice marriage of liquor to foods, even more so for desserts! We selected five meal scenarios for enjoying o-sake and desserts: as an aperitif, with brunch, at a party, in the afternoon, and as a digestive. For each of these, you can choose, marriages of o-sake and desserts with table settings according to six different moods.

The atmosphere of a meal depends on the time, place, with whom we dine, and especially the mood of the people we dine with. To enjoy meals more, we should work on table settings, as a way to create the ambience we want.

My color classification of the six moods is based on those that Mr. Robert Tisserand, a well-known aromatherapist in London, uses when he classifies essential oils according to their effects. The six types of moods are aphrodisiac, invigorating, sedative, stimulant, euphoric, and regulating.

I have managed a table coordinating school for more than a decade in Tokyo. In my school, students learn skills according to six styles based on six color classifications.

＊Reference: Psycho-Aromatherapy by Robert Tisserand 1988 ⓒTisserand Aromatherapy Ltd.

How to Find the O-sake of Your Dreams（P.006）

When you select o-sake, what clues do you use? People who choose o-sake by its ingredients and degree of rice milling must be well-experienced. I (myself) usually select o-sake by the labeling, bottle design, and name of the sake, but I can't always find the one I like using these factors.

The clue for solving this problem is in fact a very simple matter. There are only two tastes in the world: delicious or distasteful, that's what a celebrated French sommelier told me during the last class when I was studying about wines. In a nutshell, people have different tastes, so whether something is delicious or not depends on each person.

There are around 2,000 Japanese sake brewers. The number of brands is said to amount to ten thousand. If you can encounter the o-sake of your dreams, it is as lucky as if you encountered a good lover. To find the best sake, there is no better way than to search by ourselves and taste o-sake by ourselves. You can rely on advice given by professionals because it is informative, but if you want to find the o-sake of your dreams, you simply must try by yourself.

Having said so, life is too short to drink every o-sake. As a guide, you can make choices based on dryness and sweetness. By using the sake meter values, try a few types of o-sake. By comparing them, you can detect subtle differences and eventually you will find your favorite one. Your search for the sake of your dreams will get off to a good start.

Contents

Prologue	はじめに	2
Scene 1	*Prelude to Dinner* アペリティフからはじまるときめきの時間	10
Scene 2	*Enjoy Casual Brunch!* カジュアルに楽しむブランチ	26
Scene 3	*It's Party Time!* Osakeとスイーツのパーティーにようこそ！	42
Scene 4	*An Afternoon with O-sake* Osakeでアフタヌーン	58
Scene 5	*Digestif with Desserts* もうひとつの時間、ディジェスティフ	74
Scene 6	*O-sake Makers' Profiles* スイーツに似合うOsake銘鑑	90
Epilogue	おわりに	102
Index		103

[Essays]

1. Osakeとスイーツで美しく	Beauty Regimen Using O-sake and Desserts	24
2. Osakeとお米	O-sake and Rice	40
3. Hot Osakeの楽しみ方	How to Enjoy Hot O-sake	56
4. スローフードとしてのOsake	O-sake as a Slow Food	72
5. Osakeとテーブルコーディネート	O-sake and Table Settings	88

Scene 1
Prelude to Dinner

アペリティフからはじまる
ときめきの時間

食事の前に、一杯のアペリティフ(食前酒)。
仕事や家事のことは忘れ、気持ちを切り替え、胃を刺激して。
心身共に、食卓を囲む準備をします。
低アルコール酒や発泡酒など、Osakeのバラエティを楽しむチャンスです。
きれいな色のOsakeカクテルで、気分をドレスアップ。
手でつまめるフィンガーフードタイプのスイーツを添えて、
これからはじまるときめきの時間に乾杯です。

An aperitif prior to dinner will take you away
from business cares and house chores.
You can change your mood and whet your appetite.
It is a good opportunity to enjoy a variety of cocktails using o-sake
and low alcoholic beverages or sparkling sake.
Cheer yourself up with the enchanting colors of cocktails,
accompanied by finger food-type desserts.
Drink a toast to the beginning of the time for your heart to skip a beat.

白磁 長角皿(中)　玉有©
White Oblong Plate (Medium)　Gyokuyu©

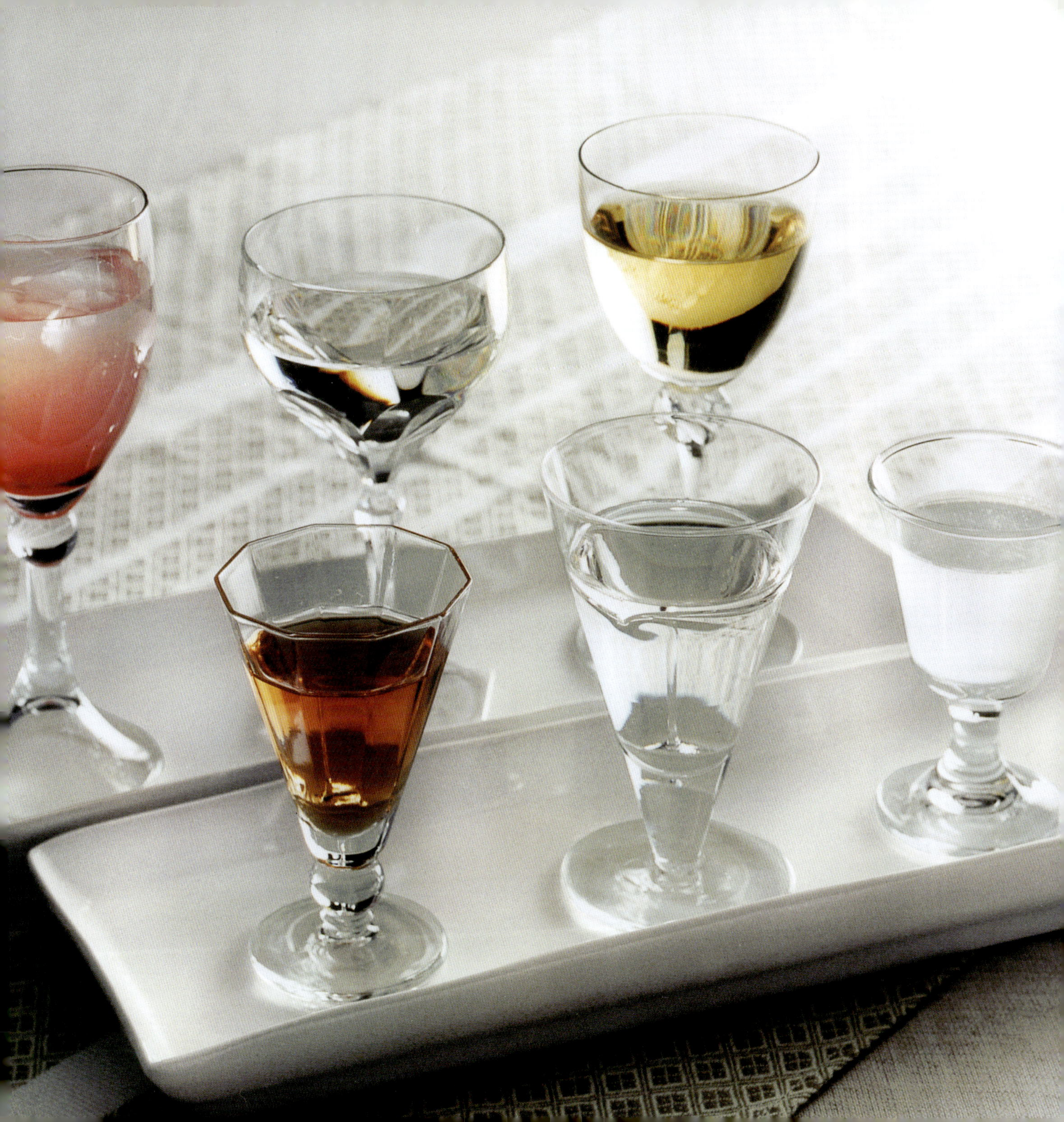

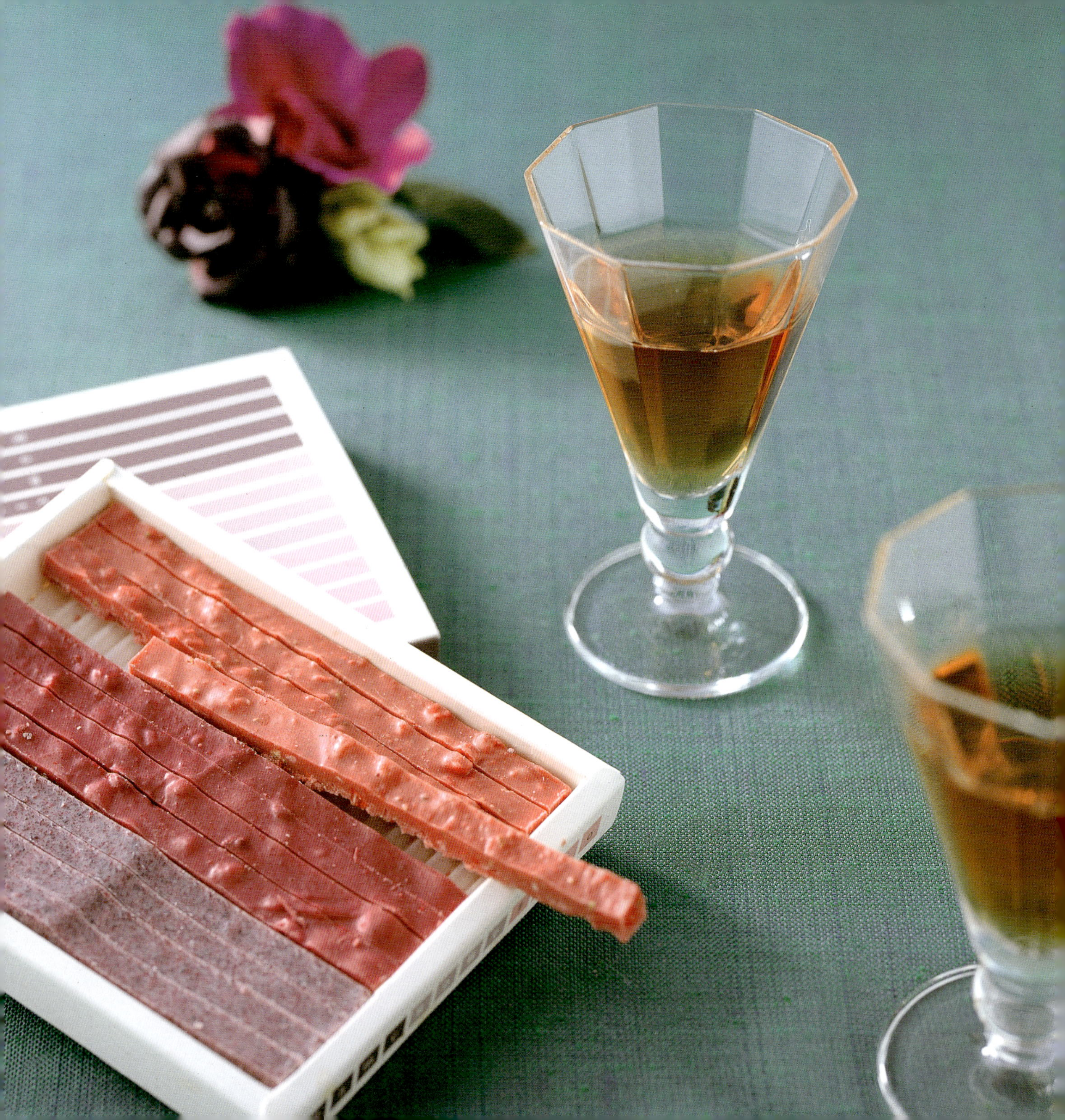

Prelude to Dinner 01

秋の紅葉を思わせる魅惑のカクテル
Osake cocktail ミスティブラウン＆スティックチョコレート

恋は美しさの秘訣。愛する人とふたりで楽しむディナーの前には、お互いの気持ちが、しっかり相手と向き合えるように、ゆったりと飲む一杯のアペリティフは欠かせません。グラスから漂う、ざくろの甘く秘めやかな香りと、スティックチョコレートから立ちのぼる濃厚なベリーの香り。Osakeカクテルの味わいとともに、あなたのなかの魅力的な一面を引き出してくれそうです。秋に色づく紅葉を思わせる、魅惑的なカクテルの色を隠し味に、これからはじまるふたりの時間への気分を高めます。

"Misty Brown" & Stick Chocolate

Love is a key to beauty. Before having a tête-à-tête dinner with a lover, a glass of aperitif is essential to sincerely listen to each other's heart. The flavor of pomegranate and the voluptuous berry aroma from the stick chocolate should bring out your romantic charms, accompanied by exotic o-sake.

色彩とイメージ
紫と深みのあるレッドカラーやグリーンの組み合わせは、成熟した、華やかでセクシーな魅力をもったおとなの女性を演出するのにふさわしいカラーです。／グラス　日本の酒情報館SAKE PLAZA Ⓐ

Color and Image
The combinations of colors such as purple and dark red or green are the perfect foil or stage direction to appeal to the gorgeous and sensual charms of a mature woman. ／Glass　SAKE PLAZA Ⓐ

スティックチョコレート
甘酸っぱいフルーツを、ホワイトチョコレートに練り込んだチョコレートスティック。ラズベリー、ブルーベリー、ストロベリーの3種の味が楽しめる。冬期のみ販売。／ラメットベリーノ　シーキューブ　丸ビル店①

Stick Chocolate
These are sticks made of white chocolate containing sweet and sour fruits. You can enjoy raspberry, blueberry, and strawberry flavors.／rametto bellino C3①

手島麻記子のOsake cocktail ミスティブラウン
レシピ：程よく冷やした吟醸酒とざくろジュースを1：1の割合で混ぜるだけ。女性ホルモンの成分でもあるエストロゲンが豊富に含まれているザクロを使ったヘルシーカクテル。

Makiko Tejima's O-sake Cocktail "Misty Brown"
Recipe:
Pour moderately chilled ginjo-shu and pomegranate juice into a bowl in the ratio of 1 to 1 and stir. Pomegranate contains a lot of estrogen. This cocktail is very healthy.

- お問い合わせ先／お酒の蔵元については、P.92〜P.100、およびスイーツや食器のメーカー、ショップについてはP.103をご覧ください。
  For details on brewers, please see P.092-100. For details on desserts and tableware makers & shops, please see P.103.
- また、特に表示のない食器等は、著者の個人蔵です。
  The tableware that is not listed on P.103 are privately owned by the author.

013

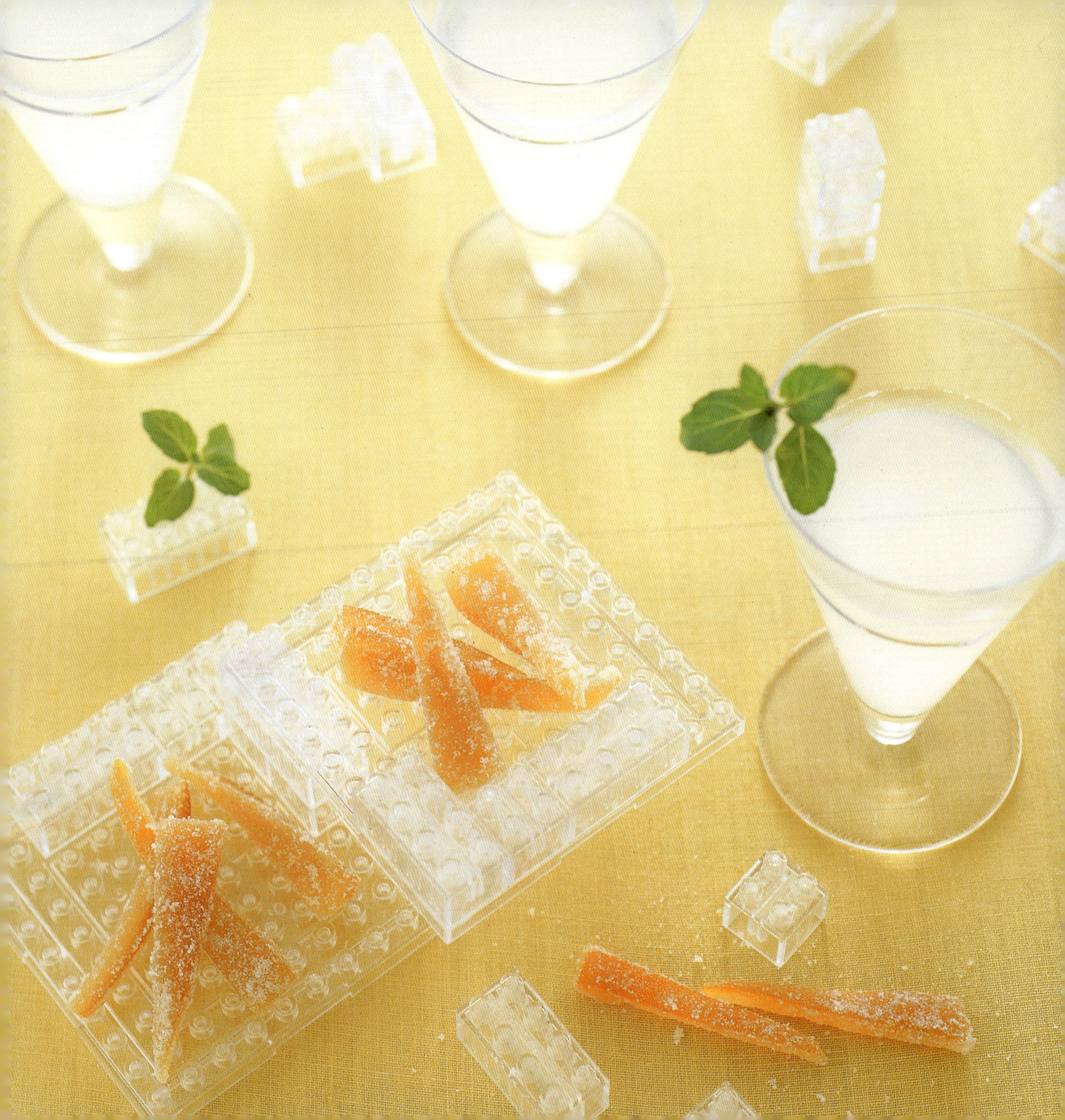

Prelude to Dinner 02

遊び心あふれるアペリティフはいかが?
RIZa &
オレンジコンフィ

友達と食事に出かける前のひととき、ちょっと家に寄ってもらって、こんな遊び心あふれるアペリティフでのおもてなしはいかがですか。ブロックを器に見たて、立体的にオレンジコンフィを盛りつけます。Osakeは、低アルコールのスパークリング純米酒。ドライな口当たりと、オレンジのさわやかな酸味が心地よく胃を刺激し、食事への期待が高まります。ミントの葉を添えて、グリーン、オレンジ、Osakeの乳白色、ブロックのクリアカラーが、さわやかな気分を演出してくれます。

RIZa & Orange Comfit

How about entertaining friends in a playful way by placing orange comfits on plates made from blocks? The low alcohol sparkling pure rice sake goes well with the dry and acidic orange taste, gently stimulating the appetite as a prelude to dinner. By garnishing with mint leaves, the combination of the green leaves and the orange comfit adds yet another note of breezy charm to the opalescent o-sake.

ブロックの器
ブロックを、器として組み立ててみると、また違った面白さを発見できます。自分だけのオリジナル食器です。／ダイヤブロック　河田①
／グラス　Sugahara⑧

Blocks (used as plates)
When constructing with various blocks, you can create your own original plates.／DIA BLOCK　KAWADA CO., LTD.①／Glass　SUGAHARA GLASSWORKS INC.⑧

オレンジコンフィ
バレンシア産の良質なオレンジを、じっくり漬け込んだコンフィは、果物の甘みと酸味の、絶妙なバランスが、後をひくおいしさです。／エモーションズ②

Orange Comfit
Comfits are made, using oranges from Valencia, soaked in syrup. The superb balance between the sweetness and acidity leaves a pleasant aftertaste. ／Favorite Co., Ltd.②

RIZa（岩手）
お米（フランス語でRiz）だけから出来た微発泡のスパークリングは、後味もさっぱり。キリリと冷して、ヴァカンスの海辺で飲む一杯は、最高に幸せな気分にしてくれます。／あさ開（P.92）

RIZa
This sparkling sake made from rice has a refreshing aftertaste. Having a glass of chilled RIZa at the beach will be blissfull.／Asabiraki Co., Ltd.（P.92）

INVIGORATING

015

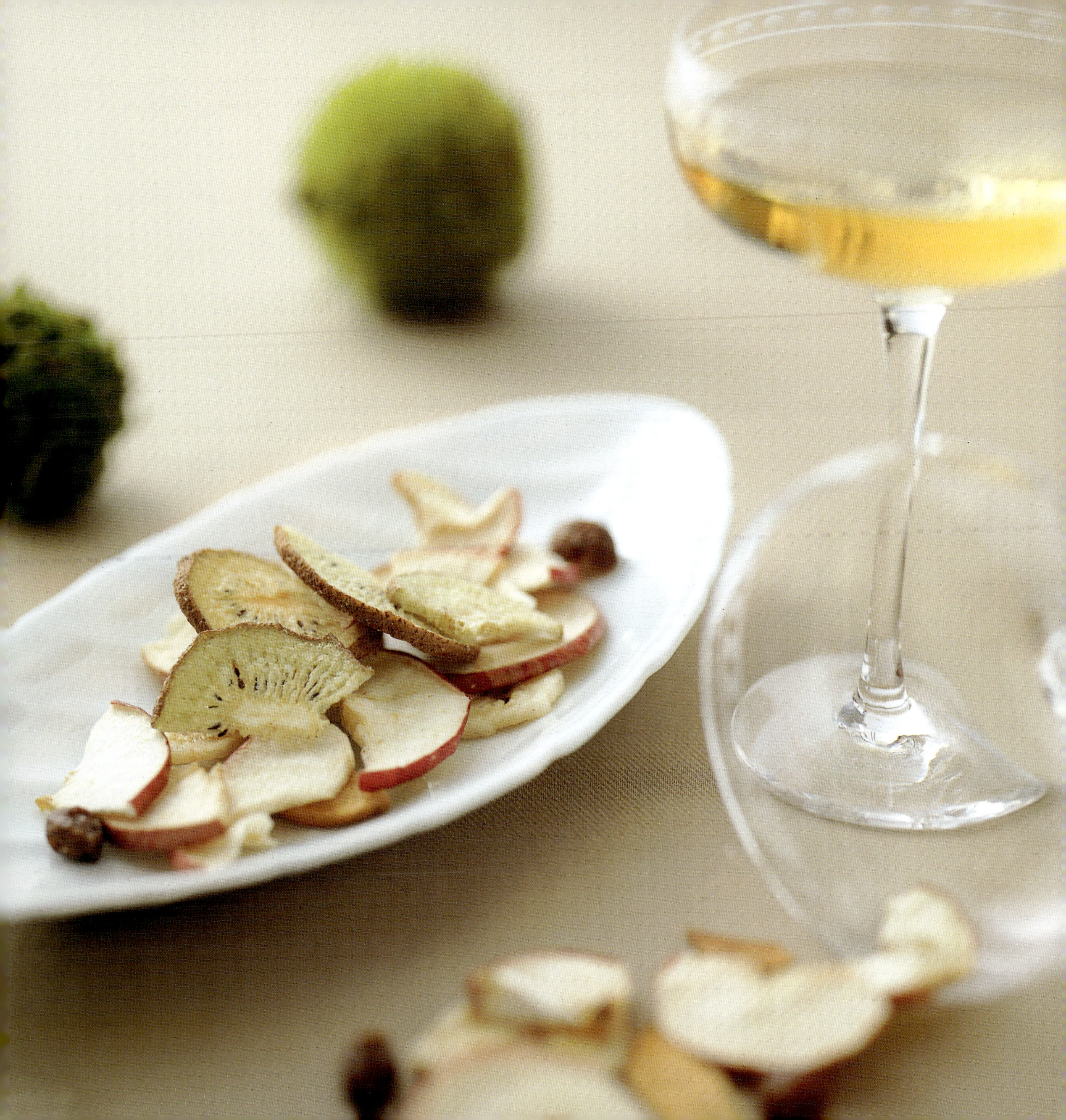

Prelude to Dinner

03

張り詰めた気持ちを緩めるさっぱりした食前酒
Osake cocktail ナチュラルガーデン&フルーツチップス

張り詰めて仕事をした日のアペリティフには、こんなさっぱりとした飲み口のカクテルがおすすめです。きりっと冷やした吟醸酒が隠し味となって、アップルジュースの甘さを上品に仕立てます。はじめて飲む人は、これがOsakeカクテルとは、きっと誰も気づかないことでしょう。気取らない自然な味わいが、フルーツチップスとよく合います。苔玉や盆栽を飾って、それまでの慌ただしかった時間から、ゆったりと気持ちを解放してあげましょう。

"Natural Garden" & Fruit Chips

After a hectic day, this clear tasting cocktail will freshen you up. The subtle flavor of o-sake bestows flavors to the sweetness of the apple juice. Some people might not notice that o-sake is present. The unpretentious natural taste goes well with fruit chips. A moss covered clay ball and a *bonsai* will help you to relax and alleviate your stress.

SEDATIVE

フルーツチップス
りんご、バナナ、キウイなど、素材のおいしさが、ぎゅっと詰まったフルーツチップス。フルーツの酸味がカクテルによく合います。

Fruit Chips
These fruit chips are made of apple, banana, kiwi, and so on. The daintiness of each fruit is condensed in the chips. They go well with fruit-flavored cocktails.

手島麻記子のOsakeカクテル ナチュラルガーデン
よく冷した吟醸酒、または大吟醸酒と、クリアタイプのアップルジュースを、グラスに2:1の割合で入れて、ステアリングするだけ。簡単に出来る、Osakeカクテルです。

Makiko Tejima's O-sake Cocktail "Natural Garden"
Pour chilled ginjo-shu or dai-ginjo-shu and golden apple juice into a glass, with a ratio of 2 parts o-sake to 1 part apple juice and then stir. It is easy to make, but tastes good.

クープシャンパングラス
女性の乳房をかたどったといわれる、広口タイプのシャンパングラスは、そのやわらかな曲線的な丸みが、やさしい気分にさせてくれます。／グラス　Sugahara Ⓑ／リーフ皿　玉有Ⓒ

Coup Champagne Glass
Having a wide mouth and shaped like a woman's breast, the curved lines of this champagne glass make us feel sensual.／Glass　SUGAHARA GLASSWORKS INC. Ⓑ／Leaf-shaped Plate　GyokuyuⓇ

017

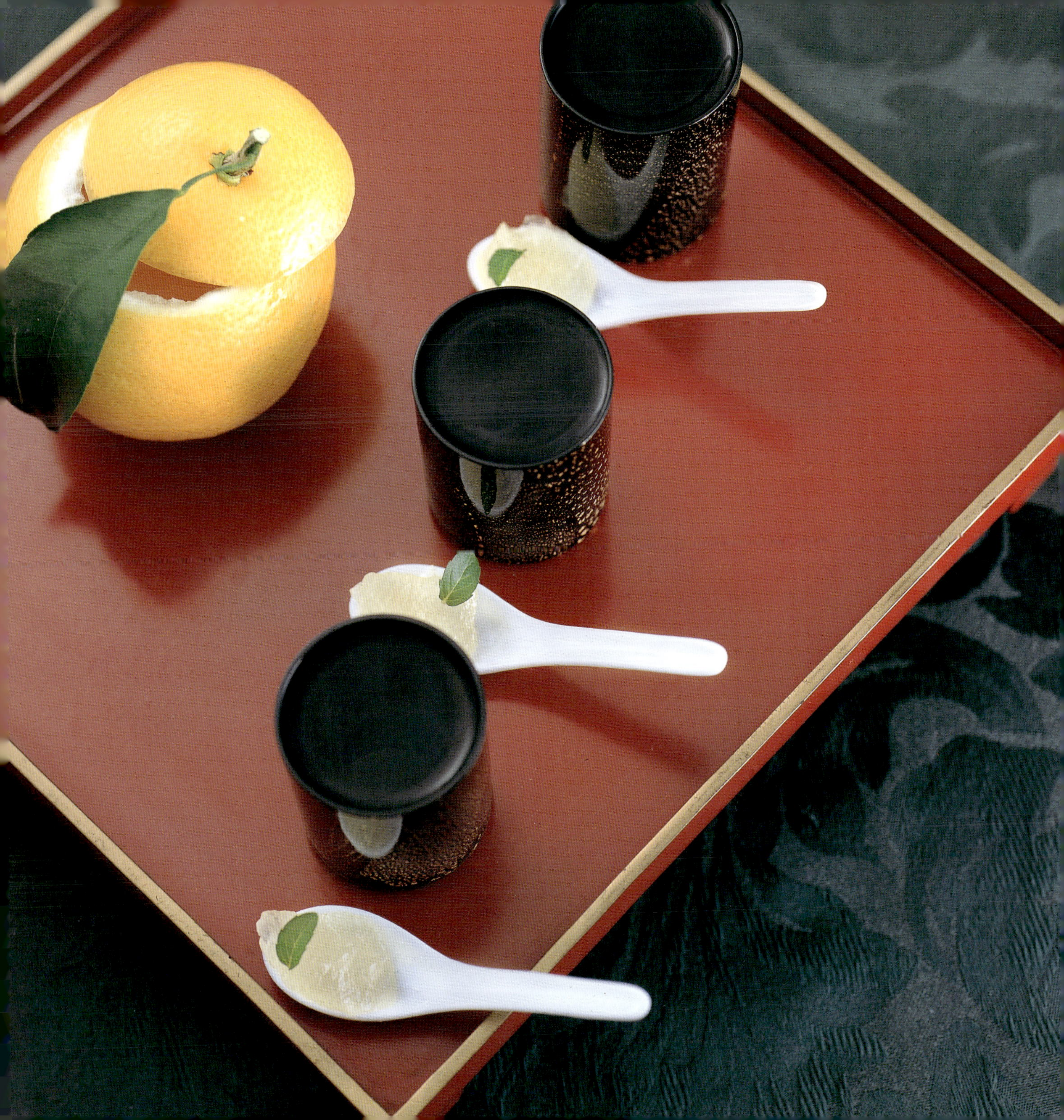

Prelude to Dinner 04

柑橘が運ぶ夏の香りで、エキゾチックに
丸眞正宗 吟の舞 & 夏みかんゼリー

アジアンフードの食卓を囲む前のひととき、朱塗りのお膳に黒のガラス製のぐい呑みとまっ白なレンゲで、エキゾチックなコントラストをしつらえます。すっきりとした口あたりの後、繊細でやわらかな甘さの余韻が広がるOsakeと新鮮な果汁100%の夏みかんゼリーが、心地よい夏の香りを運んできます。ひと口で食べられるように盛り付けたミニレンゲのゼリーには、ミントを添えて夏らしく。

Marushin Masamune Gin no Mai & Summer Orange Jelly

When you eat Asian food, place a black sake cup made of glass on a cinnabar varnished tray. Contrast this with a white porcelain spoon, and complete with mint leaves. When you drink this o-sake, you will notice its delicate, sweet aftertaste. Fresh orange juice brings you the fragrance of a comfortable summer.

朱塗りのお膳
骨董市での掘り出し物。家庭でもまだお膳で食事をすることが多かった昭和初期の頃のもの。アペリティフトレイにぴったりです。／ひな膳 漆楽Ⓓ／寸胴ぐいのみ SugaharaⒷ

Cinnabar Varnished Tray
I bought this 70-year-old tray at an antique fair. It is perfect for serving an aperitif.／Hina-zen UrushirakuⒹ／Waistless Sake-cup SUGAHARA GLASSWORKS INC.Ⓑ

夏みかんゼリー
宮崎県、高知県が主産地の、ニューサマーオレンジともいわれている柑橘の果物。柚子に似た香り高さが特徴です。2月下旬から3月下旬の限定品です。／日向夏みかんゼリー 京橋千疋屋 表参道原宿店③

Summer Orange Jelly
An orange called "New Summer Orange" is grown in Miyazaki and Kochi Prefectures. It is available only in late February and March.／Kyobashi Senbikiya (Omotesandou Harajuku Branch)③

丸眞正宗 吟の舞（東京）
フレンチのゼリー寄せ冷製前菜や、イタリアンの肉や野菜の香草風味のグリルとも合う、インターナショナルな味です。／小山酒造（P.98）

Marushin Masamune Gin no Mai
This o-sake marries nicely to French style cold jellied appetizers or Italian style grilled meats and vegetables with sweet herbs. It has an international taste.／Koyama Shuzou (P.98)

STIMULANT

019

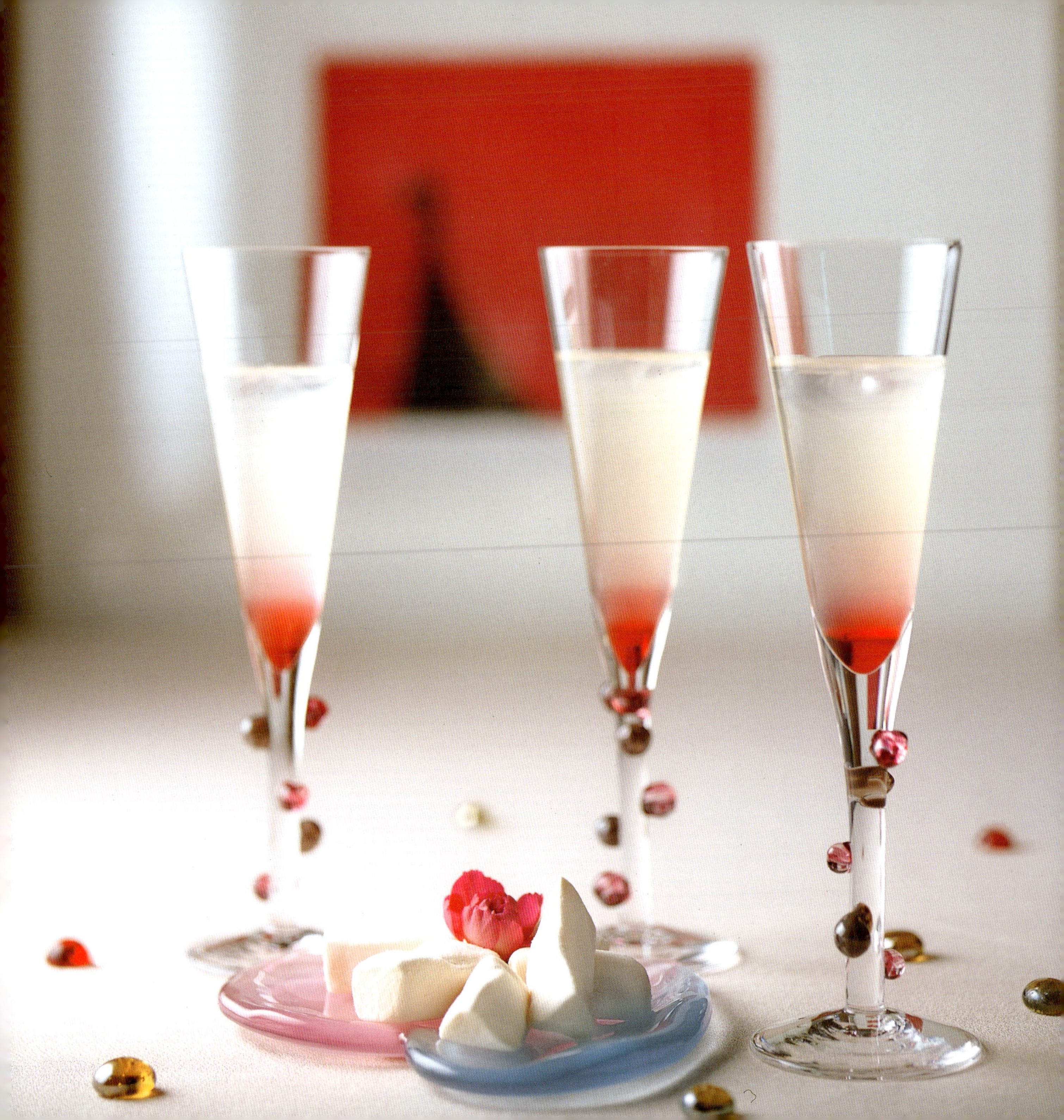

Prelude to Dinner
05

桃のカクテルとスイーツがもたらす幸せな気分
Osake cocktail プリマヴェーラ＆ピーチマシュマロ

ヴェネチアのハリーズバーで飲んだ伝説のカクテル、ベリーニのおいしさが忘れられず、ピーチ味のOsakeカクテルを作ってみました。春先や、ウエディングパーティーのアペリティフに似合う、見た目にもロマンティックな味わいのジュース感覚のカクテルです。一緒に口に入れたマシュマロが、シュワっと溶けて、口いっぱいにピーチの香りが広がり、とても幸福な気分にしてくれます。あえてステアリングせず、ピンクのグラデーションを楽しんだ後に、交ぜて飲んでください。

"Primavera" & Peach Marshmallow
Since I cannot forget the legendary Bellini cocktail I drank in Venice, I made a peach-flavored cocktail. It tastes and looks romantic. A bite of marshmallow melts in your mouth and the first sip tastes elegantly sweet. Before stirring the cocktail, enjoy the beautiful gradation of the pink colors.

フルートシャンパングラス
カクテルの色のグラデーションを楽しむのに、ぴったりの形です。ステムのガラスドロップがかわいらしいデザインです。／メヌエット Sugahara Ⓑ

Flute Champagne Glass
This glass is suitable to enjoy the color gradation of a cocktail. Marbles attached to the stem of the glass look cute.／Menuett　SUGAHARA GLASSWORKS INC. Ⓑ

ピーチマシュマロ
マシュマロがOsakeに合うかは、最初は半信半疑でしたが、意外に弾力のある触感と、さわやかなフレーバーがカクテルにぴったりです。／サワーピーチマシュマロ　日本アンカー④

Peach Marshmallow
The stronger-than-expected elasticity of marshmallows and the fresh flavor of peaches made a good marriage.／Sour Peach Marshmallow Anchor Japan Co., Ltd. ④

手島麻記子のOsake cocktail プリマヴェーラ
レシピ：ひとり分
材料：スパークリング純米酒、または純米酒50ml、ピーチフルーツミックスジュース50ml（市販されているドールのものを使っています）、グレナデンシロップ5ml（ざくろ果汁の入った赤いシロップ）、氷　適宜
作り方：氷を入れたグラスにあらかじめまぜておいたOsakeとジュースを注ぎ、最後にグレナデンシロップをスプーンで静かに入れると、比重の関係で、下に沈み、きれいなグラデーションが出来上がります。

Makiko Tejima's O-sake Cocktail "Primavera"
Recipe for a flute champagne glass : Dole's Peach Fruit Mix Juice—50ml／Sparkling junmai-shu or junmai-shu*—50ml／Grenadine syrup—5ml／First, pour the juice and then the o-sake into the glass. Then, gently add grenadine syrup. The heavy syrup will sink to the bottom of the glass and show an exquisite gradation of colors. (*Junmai-shu: This is 'pure rice' sake in which only rice, koji rice (rice malt), and water are used as ingredients, with no addition of alcohol, sugar, or anything else.)

Please see page 101.

EUPHORIC

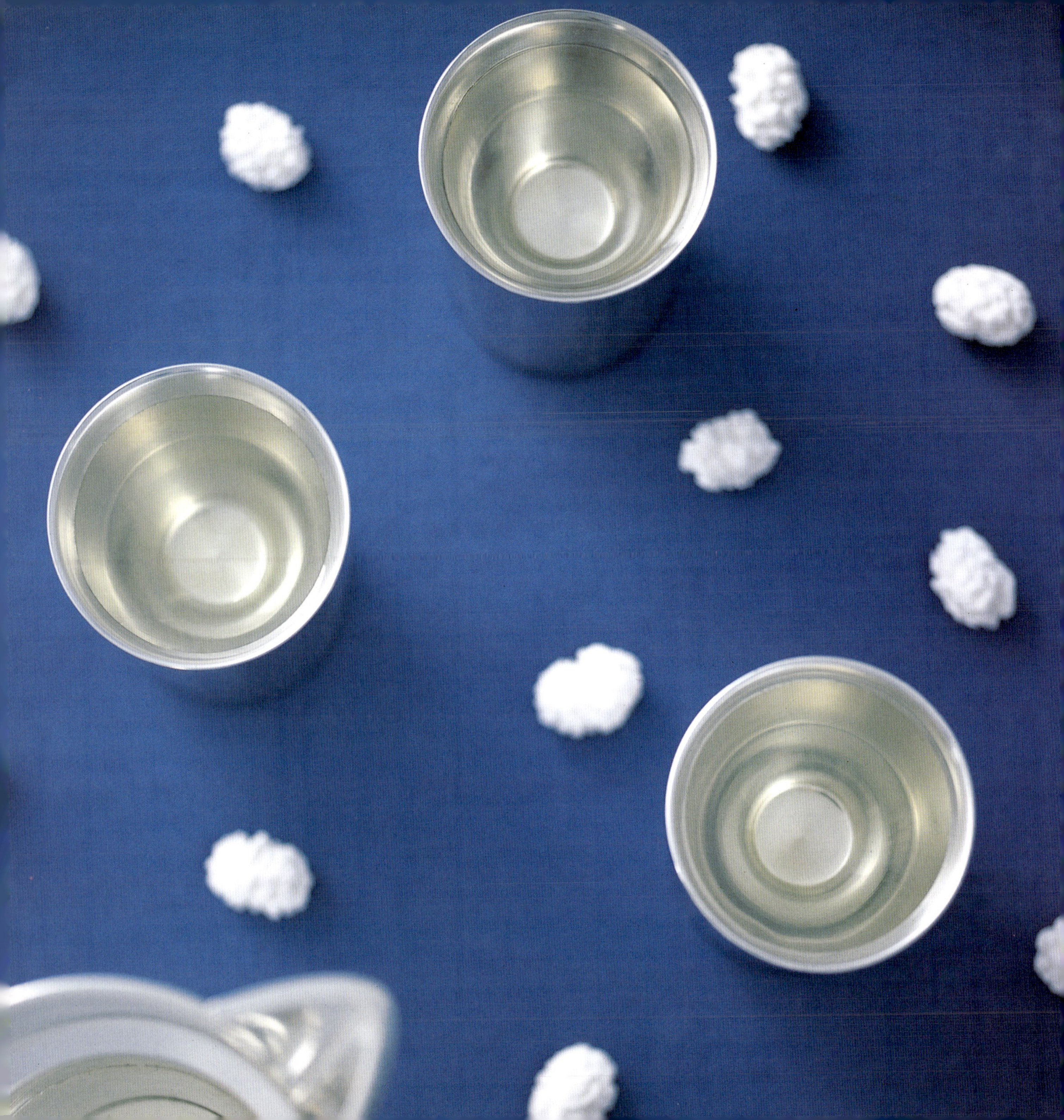

Prelude to Dinner 06

夜の海に降る牡丹雪のように、クールに
浦霞禅 & はっか豆

よく冷やした、切れ味のよい一杯のOsakeと懐かしいハッカ味のスイーツ。胃と心をスッキリほどよく刺激して、これからはじまるディナーを、待ち遠しい気分にさせてくれます。気持ちを落ち着かせるブルーカラーをベースに、錫の光沢とはっか豆のホワイトで、シンプルにコーディネート。あえてお皿は使わずに、夜の海に降る牡丹雪をイメージしてみました。アペリティフとしては、アルコール度数もかなりしっかりとしたOsakeなので、ハッカ味に誘われてくれぐれも飲み過ぎないように。

Urakasumi Zen & Mint Beans

A cup of well chilled, zesty o-sake and the refreshing flavor of mint stimulate both of your stomach and your mind. The sedative color of the dark blue tablecloth, the luster of tin cups, and the white mint-covered beans grace your table simply. The mint beans look like large flakes of snow falling on the sea at midnight. This o-sake is strong. Please be sure not to drink too much.

錫製のカップ
中空で二重構造になっているカップは、本来燗酒を飲むものですが、手の温度が伝わりにくいので、冷して飲むOsakeの味も、いい状態に保ちます。／上燗コップ、タンポ共に大阪錫器Ⓔ

Cup Made of Tin
This cup is usually used to warm up o-sake. It is insulated so it is comfortable to hold when it contains hot o-sake. And, this cup keeps cold o-sake cool.／Jokan Cup and Tampo* Osaka Suzuki Co., Ltd. Ⓔ

*Tampo: Pitcher for heating o-sake.

はっか豆
北海道の北見は、過去、世界の70％のミント栽培を誇った地方です。道産大豆を雪のようにまっ白に包み込んだ、北国のお菓子です。／北見ハッカ通商⑤

Mint Beans
Kitami's mint production once accounted for 70% of mint production in the world. Locally grown beans are covered with white mint like snow.／Kitami Hakka Tsusho Co., Ltd. ⑤

浦霞禅（宮城）▲
味噌の風味とよく合うOsakeです。田楽はもちろん、小さく切ったブルーチーズに柚子味噌をのせたつまみとも、なかなかいけます。／佐浦（P.93）

Urakasumi Zen
This o-sake matches a miso (salt added to fermented soy beans; soy sauce is made from miso) flavor. It also goes well with dengaku served with miso sauce.
*Dengaku: spit-roasted meat, tofu, vegetables, or konnyaku (a jelly type food made of konnyaku potatoes).／Saura Co., Ltd. (P.93)

023

Scene 2

Enjoy Casual Brunch!

カジュアルに楽しむブランチ

心おきなく朝寝坊をした休日は、やわらかな陽射しを浴びて、
ブランチを。朝食と昼食をかねたブランチメニューに欠かせない焼き菓子と、
Osakeを合わせ、ゆったりと過ごすくつろぎの時間。テラスにテーブルを出し、
庭に咲く花を飾りましょう。手触りもナチュラルな枡で飲むOsakeからは、
檜の香りがほんのりと漂い、日頃の忙しさから解放され、
心身ともに、リラックスして楽しむひとときです。

After a nice sleep-in on a holiday, enjoy a lazy brunch outside.
If you have baked cakes with o-sake served in *masu**,
the flavor of cypress and the comfortable touch of wood
will release you from the stresses of everyday life.

蜜のケーキ 木風⑥／長角銚子 玉有Ⓒ／カメリアプレート SugaharaⒷ／ル・ジャカール・フランセ テーブルクロス　ケイズ・コンポジションⓊ
Maple Syrup Cake　KIKAZE⑥／Square Sake Pitcher　GyokuyuⒸ
／Camellia Plate　SUGAHARA GLASSWORKS INCⒷ／Tablecloth　LE JACQUARD FRANÇAISⓊ

*Masu are made of wood, such as Japan cedar or Japan cypress. Masu were originally
used for measuring liquid volume, but nowadays they are used as cups, too.

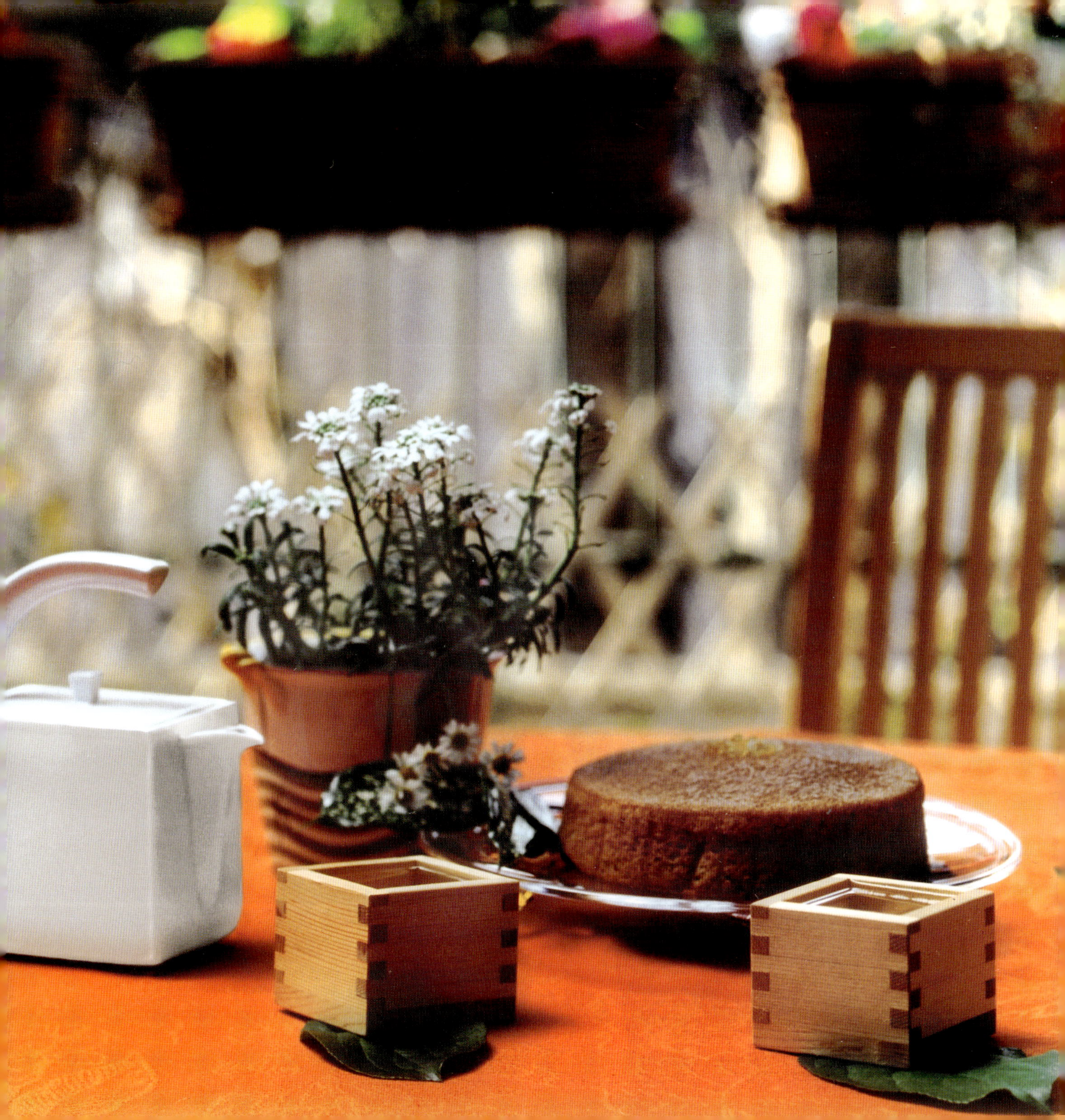

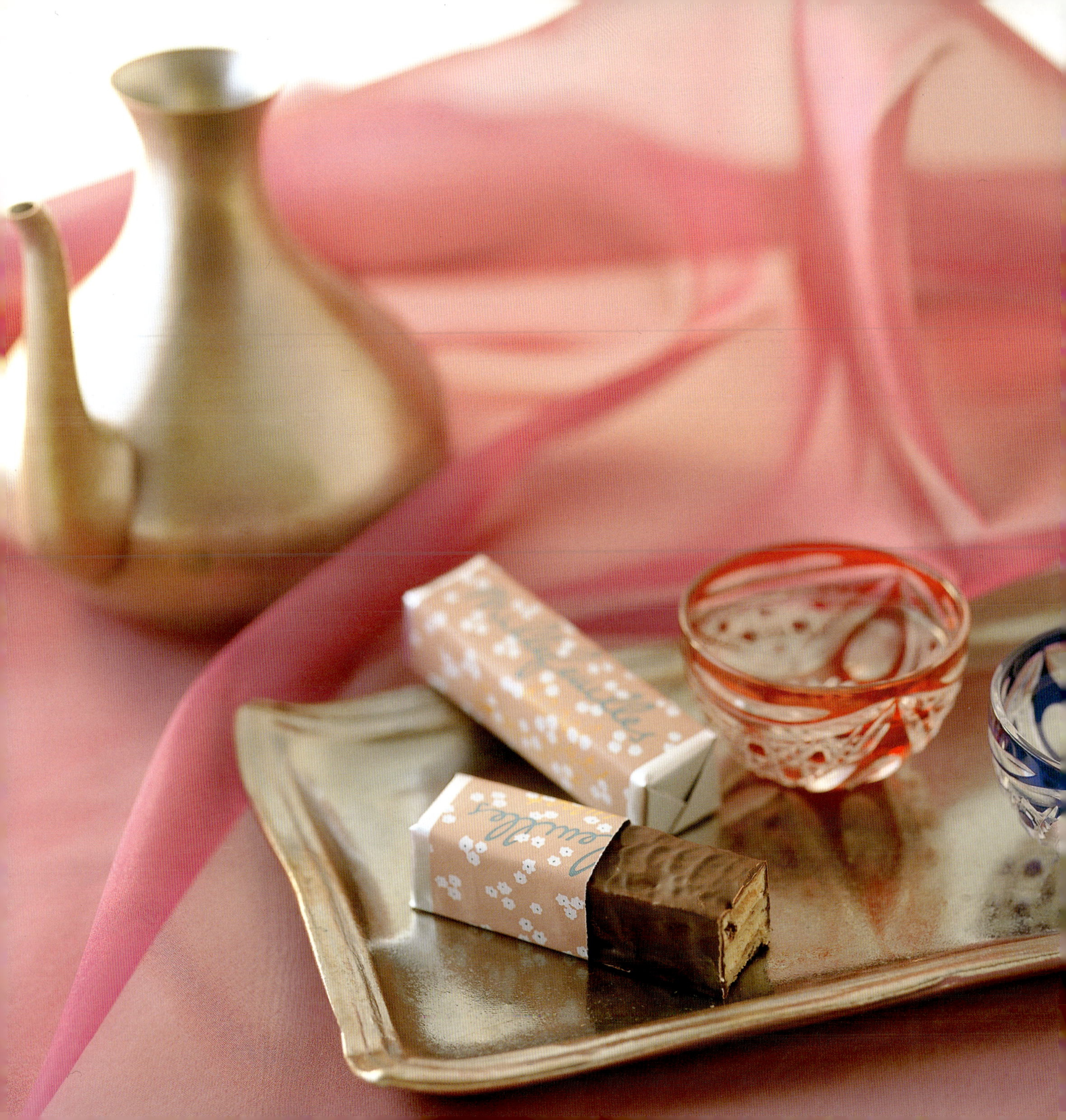

APHRODISIAC

Enjoy Casual Brunch!
07

甘美へと誘う、夢見心地の時間を演出
大吟醸 霊泉汲不盡 (レイセンクメドモツキズ) &
ミルフィユ

時間を気にせずに過ごせる、贅沢な休日のはじまりには、グラスから立ち昇るOsakeのふっくらとした甘い香りがよく似合います。ハイミルクチョコレートに包まれたサクっとしたパイが、ふくよかな味のOsakeと共にクリーミーに溶け合って、甘美な世界へと誘います。やわらかな曲線のフォルムが美しい徳利は、Osakeの産地と同じ新潟県の伝統工芸品の鎚起銅器です。テーブルには、一枚の優美な色のヴェールをまとわせ、ふたりの夢見心地の時間を演出します。

Reisen Kumedomo Tsukizu & Mille-feuille

When you do not have to work against the clock, the sweet and soft flavor of this o-sake complements the situation. The crispy pie of the mille-feuille coated with milk chocolate goes well with the o-sake. This curvy copper *tokkuri* is a local traditional handicraft. Both the o-sake and the tokkuri come from Niigata Prefecture. A graceful dark red sheer tablecloth serves as a foil for stardust time.

切子のグラス
カットグラスともいわれる切子の文様は、光を受けて、Osakeを注いだグラス越しに、ゆらゆらとテーブルに微妙な陰影をつくり出します。／盃　東京カットグラス工業協同組合Ⓖ／徳利一献（いっこん）玉川堂Ⓕ

Cut Glass
The patterns inscribed on the glass throw delicate wavy shadows on the table.／Glass　Cooperative Association of Tokyo Cut Glass KogyoⒼ／Tokkuri Ikkon　GYOKUSENDO CO., LTD.Ⓕ

ミルフィユ
1965年より作られているロングセラーのスイーツ。ハイミルク、スイート、ヘーゼルナッツの3種類の味が楽しめる。7月中旬より9月末まで、配送は休止。／ベルンのミルフィユ　ベルン⑦

Mille-feuille
This has been produced since 1965, a long selling item. You can enjoy high milk, sweet and hazel nut flavors. These mille-feuille cakes are available from mid-July through September.／Berne Co., Ltd. ⑦

大吟醸 霊泉汲不盡（新潟）（レイセンクメドモツキズ）
炊きたてのご飯を口にしたときのような、ふわっとした甘い風味は、たらの芽のてんぷらなど、生命の息吹を感じさせる春の山菜料理などによく合います。／白瀧酒造（P.96）

Reisen Kumedomo Tsukizu
When drinking this o-sake, I am reminded of rice boiled to the perfect degree of softness. It matches wild vegetables and causes us to feel the coming of spring buds.／SHIRATAKI SAKE BREWERY CO., LTD. (P.96)

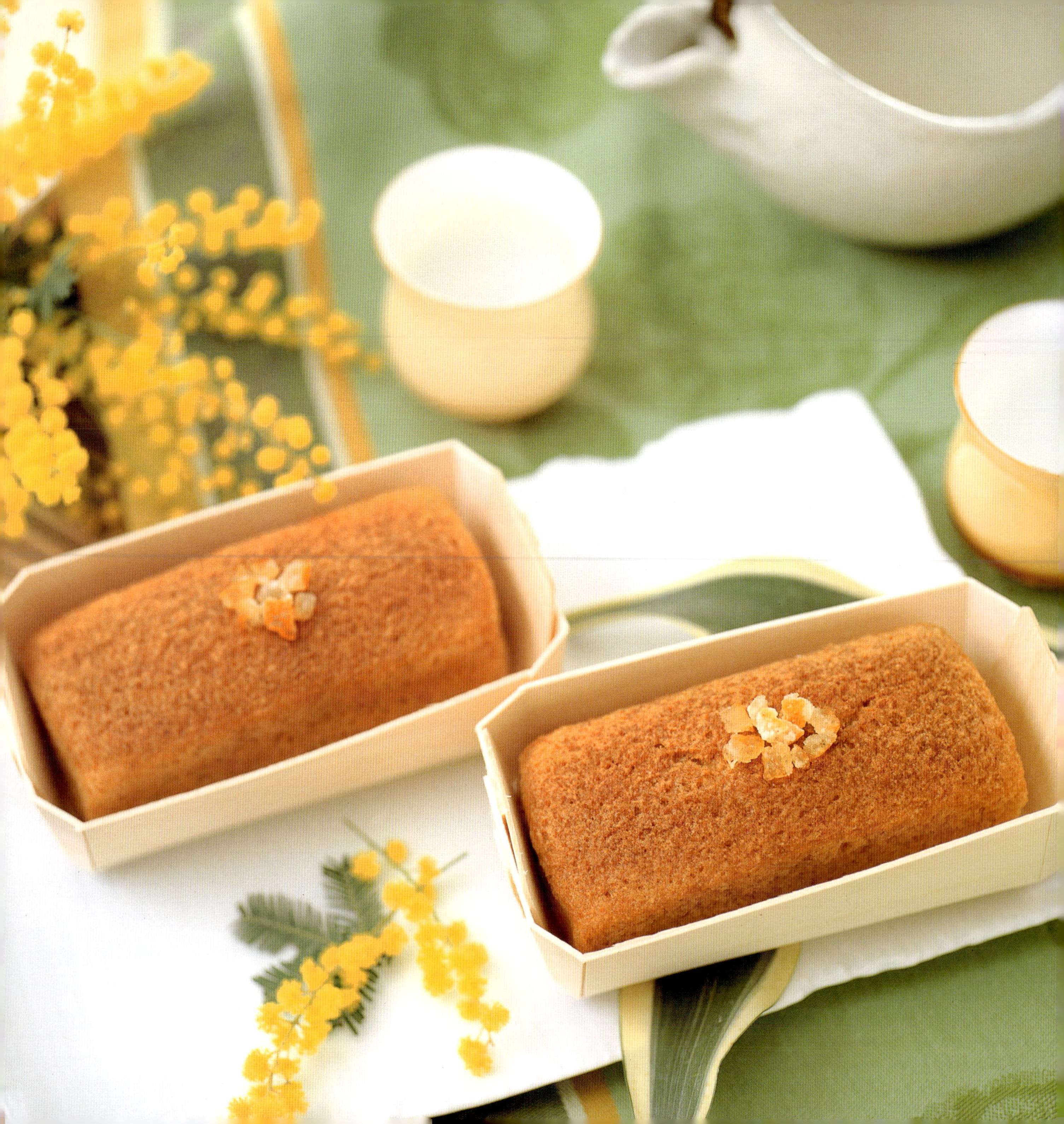

Enjoy Casual Brunch! 08

さわやかなハーモニーを奏でる、休日のブランチ
純米 上善如水 &
蜜のケーキ

鮮やかなイエローやグリーンは、元気をくれるビタミンカラー。まっ白なお皿に、良質なメイプルシロップがしっとりと溶け込んだケーキを盛り付けて、ミモザの花をあしらいます。ふくよかでありながらすっきりとした味わいの純米酒が、スイーツのナチュラルな甘さと柚子の風味と共に、さわやかなハーモニーを奏でます。何となく元気のでない休日は、こんなブランチで気分を明るく、楽しく変えて、公園にでも、出かけてみませんか。

Junmai Jozen Mizu no Gotoshi & Maple Cake

Place a piece of cake on a white plate, decorating with mimosa. The vivid colors of yellow and green energize us. The full-bodied, but light, taste of junmai-shu (sake made of pure rice) creates harmony with the flavor of citron and the natural sweetness of the cake. When you feel downbeat, cheer yourself up with a brunch like this.

片口の器
かつては、酒樽や醤油樽から、中身を瓶に移し換えるために使われていた片口。酒器として食卓で使うと、たっぷりと空気に触れた、まろやかな味のお酒が楽しめます。／白磁流木長角皿 玉有Ⓒ／ル・ジャカール・フランセ テーブルランナー ケイズ・コンポジションⓊ

Lipped Sake-vessel
Lipped vessels were originally used to transfer o-sake or soy sauce from barrels. Lipped vessels give a wider exposure of o-sake to air and bring a mellow flavor./White Porcelain Raft-shaped Square Plate GyokuyuⒸ/Table Runner LE JACQUARD FRANÇAISⓊ

蜜のケーキ
きめ細やかに焼き上げられた生地に、たっぷりと浸みこんだメイプルシロップ。その自然な甘さが、何ともいえないやさしい味のケーキです。／"木風"オリジナル小さい蜜のケーキ（柚子メイプル） 木風⑥

Maple Cake
The fine texture of this cake is glazed with abundant maple syrup. The natural sweetness is striking./KIKAZE.⑥

純米 上善如水（新潟）
瓶ラベルの色は、食欲増進効果のあるオレンジカラー。どんな料理ともよく合う、普段の食卓にぴったりのOsakeです。／白瀧酒造（P.96）

Junmai Jozen Mizu no Gotoshi
The orange color of the bottle's label enhances our appetite. This o-sake goes with any kind of food. It is good for casual dining./SHIRATAKI SAKE BREWERY CO., LTD(P.96)

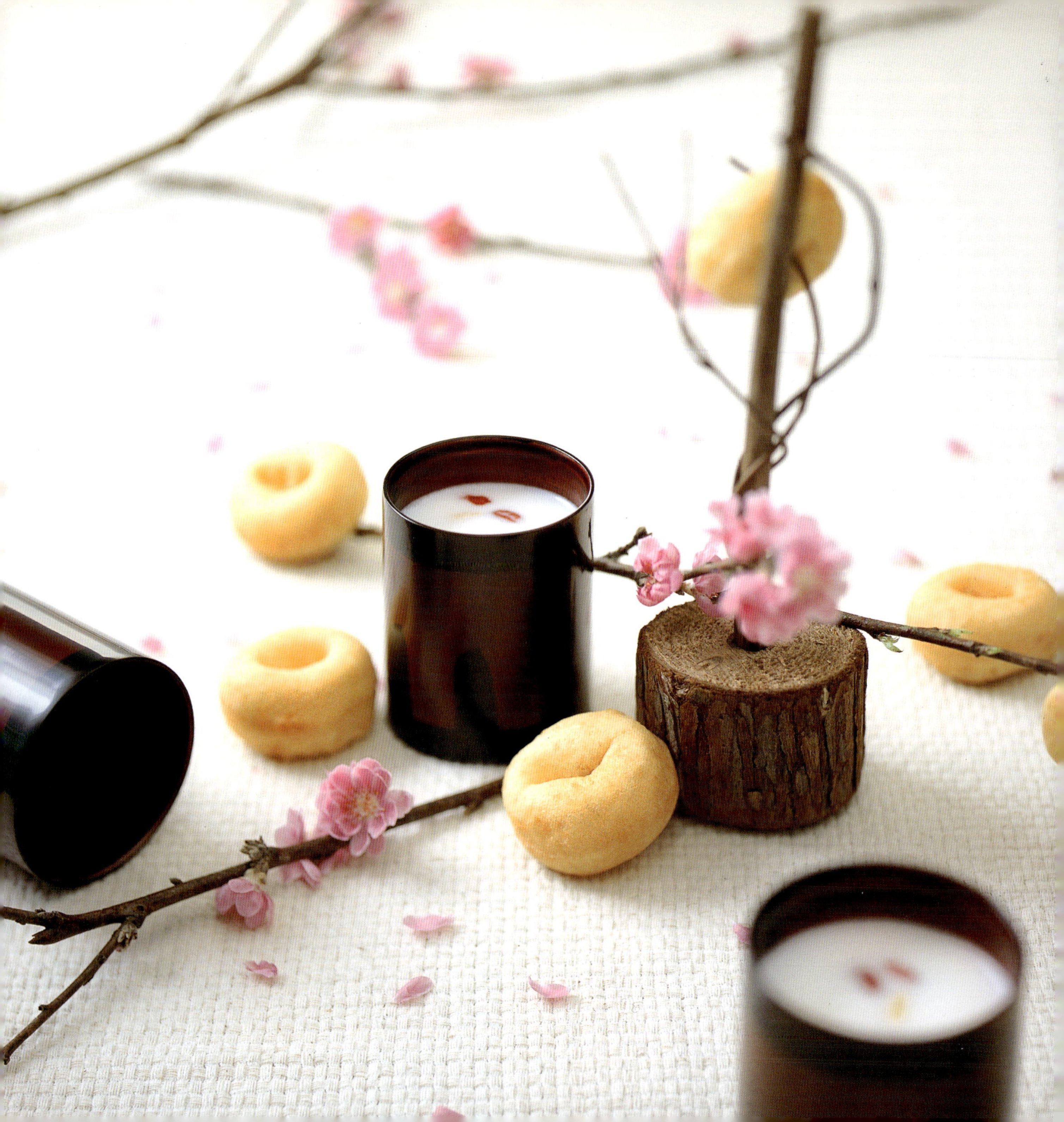

Enjoy Casual Brunch! 09

薬膳風ホットカクテルで、身も心も疲労回復
Osake cocktail "Fou-"（ふー）＆
豆乳ドーナツ

カラダもココロも、ほっくりと暖まりたい日には、部屋着のままで、ゆったりヘルシーブランチを。薬膳では食べ物を、熱性のものを「陽」、寒性のものを「陰」として5つに分類しています。この陰と陽のバランスをとることがとても重要とされています。体を温めるOsakeをベースに、「陽」に属する杏の種をパウダー状にした杏仁霜と松の実、心身の疲労回復に効果があるといわれているクコの実を入れた薬膳風ホットカクテルです。豆乳ドーナツが、口のなかでしっとりと溶け合います。

"Fou-" & Soy Milk Doughnuts
When you want to ease into the day, eat a healthy brunch, and relax in a housecoat. The balance of yin (coolness) and yang (warmth) of food is important, according to traditional Chinese herbal medicine. Based on the hot o-sake, add apricot kernel powder, pine seeds, and matrimony (boxthorn) vine seeds. This matches with the doughnut and creates harmony in the palate.

墨春慶塗りの器
木曽桧の曲げ物のカップは、手で持ったときのおさまりが心地よく、使うごとに味わいを増します。白木地の段階で墨で絵を描き、木曽春慶塗りに仕上げています。／ちきりやⒽ

Sumi Shunkei Lacquerware Cup
Every time we put a Kiso cypress lacquerware cup in our hands, we feel tranquil. This cup was painted with Japanese ink when the wood was white and then finished with Kiso Shunkei coating./Chikiriya Inc.Ⓗ

豆乳ドーナツ
揚げ菓子ながら、油っぽさが感じられず豆乳のほのかな甘さが、懐かしい味わいを醸し出しています。1袋（8個入り）200円という値段は、とってもお値打ちです。／京とうふ藤野⑧

Soy Milk Doughnuts
Although it is a fried snack, I do not feel it is oily. The slight scent of soy milk makes us feel relieved. Eight doughnuts sell for the reasonable price of 200 yen./Kyotofu Fujino⑧

手島麻記子のOsake cocktail "Fou-"
レシピ：ひとり分
材料：純米酒または純米吟醸酒45ml／牛乳60ml／杏仁霜 小さじ1（すりきり）／クコの実とマツの実 各2個
作り方：材料を耐熱性の器に全部入れ、人肌程度になるように、電子レンジで1〜2分温める。様子を見ながらくれぐれも、沸騰させないように。

Makiko Tejima's O-sake Cocktail "Fou-"
Recipe for one person:
Ingredients: Junmai-shu or junmai-ginjo-shu 45ml/Milk 60ml/Apricot kernel powder: level spoonful/Boxthorn seeds and pine seeds: 2 seeds each
How to prepare:
Put all the ingredients in a heat-resistant dish and warm it up for 1 to 2 minutes in a microwave oven. The important thing is to check the temperature of the mixture and not to bring it to the boil.

SEDATIVE

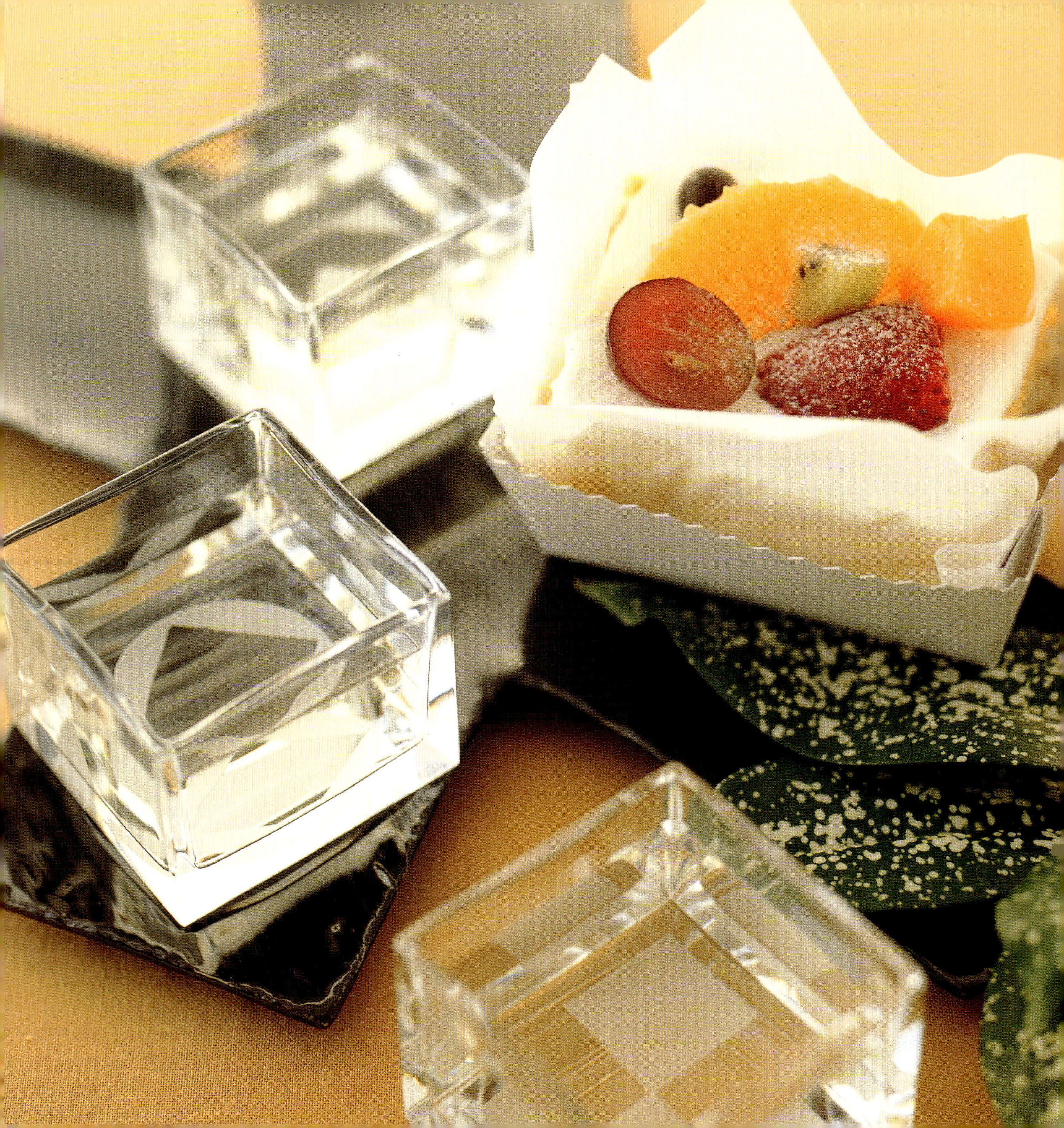

Enjoy Casual Brunch!
10

お米とそのエキスで、からだをいたわる
一ノ蔵 米米酒 & フルーツケーキ

お米をテーマにしたブランチです。このOsakeは、米と米こうじに加え、お米から抽出した体をいたわる成分、「ライスパワーエキス」を原料とした、低アルコール酒です。とろりとしたなめらかな口あたりが、米粉を使ったもっちりとしたケーキのスポンジと生クリームによく合います。四角いケーキの形に合わせ、ガラス製の枡にOsakeを注ぎ、黒のクロスプレートに斑入りのドラセナの葉っぱをあしらって食卓へ。黒、グリーン、テーブルクロスの芥子色の3色が基調になって、ケーキの色とりどりのフルーツを、エキゾチックに引き立てます。

Komekome Shu & Fruit Cake
The theme of this brunch is rice. This o-sake is not only made from rice and rice malt, but also from the nutrients in rice. It is low alcohol sake. The thick and smooth palate marries to the whipped cream and moist sponge cake made from rice powder. To coordinate with the square-shaped cakes, pour o-sake into masu-shaped glass cups, garnished with variegated leaves. The poppy orange color, green leaves, and black plates make an exotic ambience.

ガラス製の枡
ひとつずつ違う、枡の底に描かれた幾何学模様が、Osakeを注ぐとくっきりと浮き上がり、Myグラスとしても楽しめます。／半合枡グラス　HOYA（株）クリスタルカンパニー①／クロスプレート　玉有ⓒ

Masu Made of Glass
Different geometric designs are carved into the bottom of each glass. When you pour o-sake, you can enjoy the designs.／Half-sized Masu Made of Glass HOYA CORPORATION Crystal Company①／X-shaped Plate　Gyokuyuⓒ

フルーツケーキ
バットに入ったケーキを切り分けて売っているフレッシュな味は、持ち帰り時間に要注意。マスカルポーネ入りのクリームが溶けないように。6月中旬まで販売。／フルッティフルッティ　シーキューブ 丸ビル店①

Fruit Cake
Please consume this cake before the fresh cream contained mascarpone begins melting. This cake is available until mid-June.／Frutti Frutti　C³①

一ノ蔵 米米酒（宮城）
Osakeが全く飲めないと言っていた人が、これを飲んで自分にも飲めるOsakeがあったと、喜んでくれます。アルコールに弱い人におすすめです。／一ノ蔵（P.94）

Komekome Shu
Even very moderate drinkers can enjoy this.／Ichinokura Co., Ltd.(P.94)

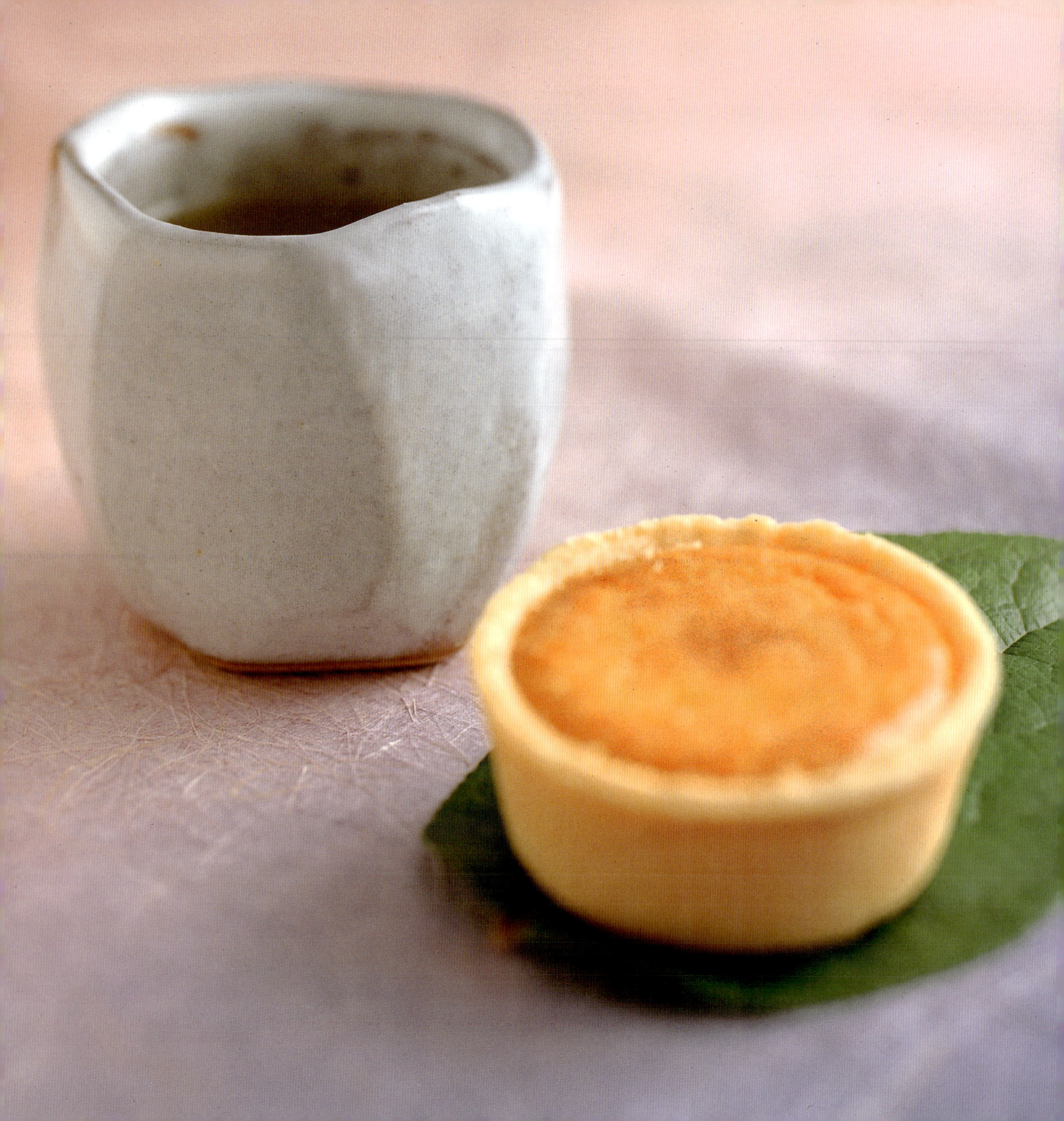

Enjoy Casual Brunch!
11

土の器と懐かしい甘酒の香りで、小さな幸せ
やんわり＆
エダムチーズケーキ

きりっと冷やして、とろりと味わう甘口のOsake。掌(てのひら)にすっぽりおさまる萩焼きのぐい呑みに注ぐと、懐かしい甘酒の香りが広がります。土の器のぬくもりと「やんわり」としたOsakeの味わいは、普段は気付かない、暮らしのなかに埋もれた、小さな幸せを感じさせてくれます。コクがありながらさっぱりとした後味のチーズケーキの酸味は、口のなかでOsakeの甘みとやさしく溶け合います。当たり前のようにいつもそばにいる家族と一緒に、ときには、そのかけがいのない幸せを、ゆっくり味わってみませんか。

Yanwari &
Edam Cheesecake

It is sweet and best chilled. When pouring this o-sake into a Hagi ware cup, a sweet bouquet is brought out. The warmth of the earthenware reminds us of the daily happiness we miss. The rich and light aftertaste of the cheesecake matches the sweetness of the o-sake. Why don't you spend some pleasurable time with your family?

白萩くりぬきぐい呑み
陶土をくりぬき、登り窯で、時間をかけてじっくりと焼きあげた器です。一点ずつ違う、なんとも愛らしい表情が、気持ちをなごませます。／船崎窯⑨

White Hagi Ware
It is made in an ascending kiln and takes a long time. Each piece of pottery has its own lovely expression. ／Funasaki-gama⑨

エダムチーズケーキ
オーストラリア産のクリームチーズをベースに、オランダ産のエダムチーズをたっぷりと使ったケーキは、葉っぱにのってしまうほどのミニサイズながら、味はしっかり本格的。／エダムチーズケーキミニ　モロゾフ⑨

Edam Cheesecake
This cake is made from Australian cream cheese and Dutch Edam cheese. It is so small that it can be placed on a leaf. The taste is remarkable and authentic.／Edam Cheesecake Mini　Morozoff⑨

やんわり（長野）
ほんの一瞬だけ火を通した、フレッシュなフォアグラと合わせてみたら…非日常的なシーンでも飲んでみたくなる、はっきりとした個性のあるOsakeです。／武重本家酒造（P.97）

Yanwari
It has a very individual taste and is sure to be nice with slightly roasted fresh foie gras. It is perfect for special occasions.／Takeshige Honke Brewing Corp (P.97)

EUPHORIC

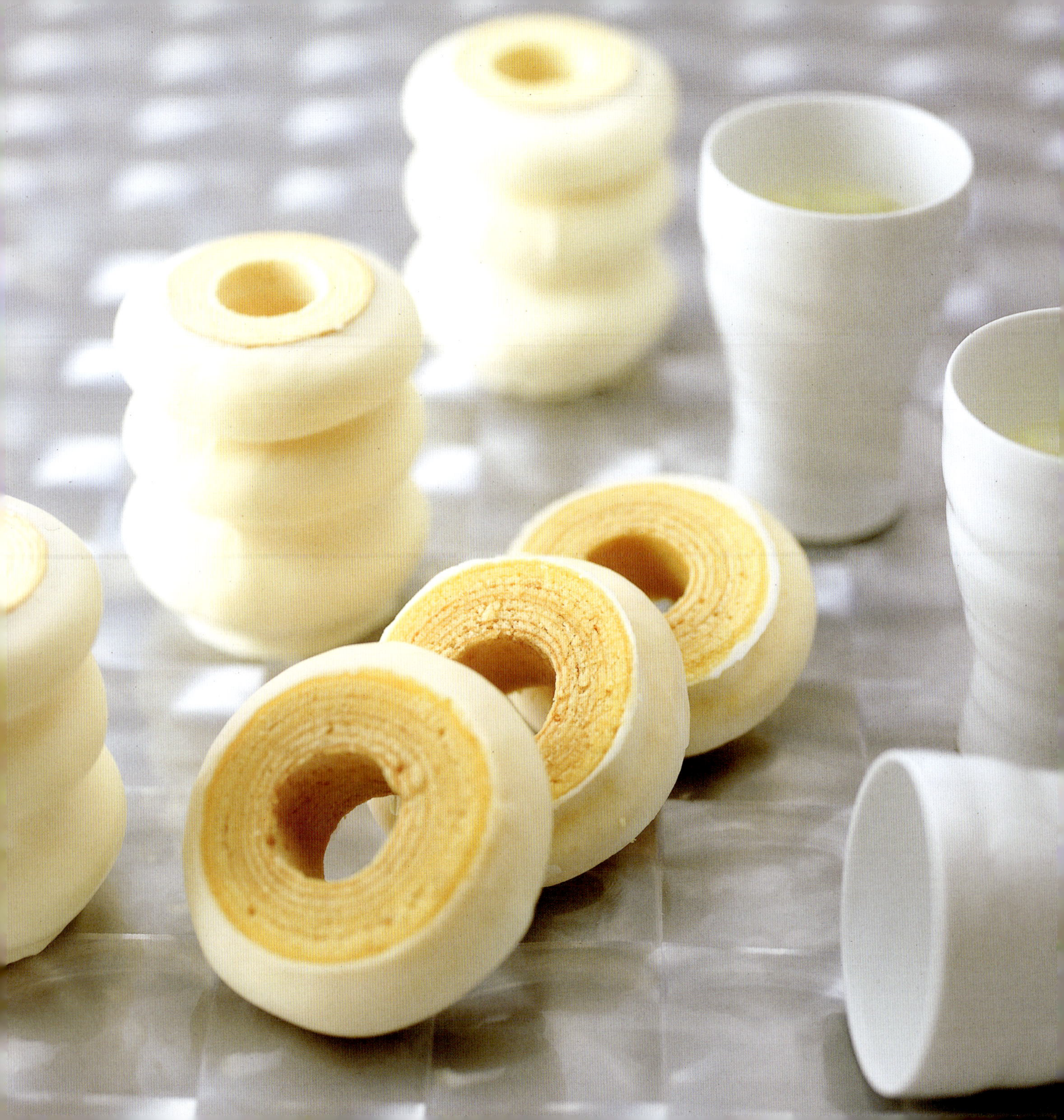

Enjoy Casual Brunch!
12

モダンアート感覚で、伝統とスタイリッシュの融合
純米大吟醸 毛利公 &
バウムクーヘン

Osakeとスイーツを、モダンアート感覚で楽しむブランチです。アルコール度数の高い、伝統的なしっかりとした味わいのOsakeを、スタイリッシュな装いをした伝統的なスイーツと合わせると、双方とも、今までとは違ったひと味を醸し出します。どちらも、素材にこだわった本格派。長い年月を経てなお、愛され続けられている伝統の味というのは、常に新しい無限大の可能性を秘めていることに気付かされます。「新しさ」ということに思いを巡らす、静かで豊かな休日のひとときです。

Junmai Dai-ginjo Mouri-Kou & Baum Kuchen

This is a brunch where you can enjoy o-sake and desserts with a modern artistic sense. This strong, traditional o-sake and this stylish dessert merge to create a unique harmony. The authentic and traditional tastes are well-received, confirming the test of times, and contain infinite possibilities.

白磁の器
日本が世界に誇る伝統的な有田焼の産地においても、日々刺激的な「新しさ」が生まれています。きめの細かい、眩しいほどの白い地肌です。／白磁 果実酒杯 玉有ⓒ

White Porcelain Ware
The town of Arita, Kyushu has world famous Arita-ware, and boasts of a long tradition. Innovative designs have been created for years. Its fine texture and brilliantly white color look appealing./White Porcelain Cup for Drinking Fruit Liquor　Gyokuyuⓒ

バウムクーヘン
伝統的なヨーロピアンスイーツが、長い年月を経て、日本の味としてしっかりと根付いているのは、純正自然のおいしさの追求の結果に違いありません。／キンダーバウムユーハイム⑩

Baum Kuchen
Although this is a traditional European dessert, it has been deeply rooted in Japanese food culture. This attainment has derived from the results of unrelenting search for excellent taste./Kinder Baum Juchheim Co., Ltd.⑩

純米大吟醸 毛利公 （山口）
洗練されながら、しっかりとした骨太な味わいは、フレンチスタイルに仕上げたヴェトナム料理などにも合います。／山縣本店 （P.100）

Junmai Dai-ginjo Mouri-Kou
It is sophisticated but has substance. It goes well with French style Vietnamese cuisine. ／Yamagata Honten (P.100)

REGULATING

Essay

Osakeとお米

「わたしたちイタリアのお米でOsakeが造れますか？」。2002年の秋、イタリアのトリノで、スローフード協会が主催する食の祭典「サローネ・デル・グスト」で、日本全国の銘酒を紹介したときのことです。ヨーロッパ産のお米の8割近くを生産するピエモンテ州の、米生産者からの質問でした。日本には、Osakeの原料として使用されているお米の代表的な品種として、「山田錦」、「五百万石」、「美山錦」、「雄町」などの素晴らしいお米が生産されています。

これら酒造りに適したお米は、「酒造好適米」と呼ばれ、普段私たちが食べているお米に比べ、粒と白い芯の部分（心白）が大きく、たんぱく質の含有量が少ないという3つの条件を揃えています。さらに、これらのお米の、玄米の胚芽や表層部に多く含まれるたんぱく質、脂肪、ミネラル、ビタミンなどの栄養素は、多すぎるとかえって、Osakeの味や香り、色調などを損ねてしまうことから、酒造りの際に高度に精米されます。普段食べているお米の精米歩合が92％程度に対して、Osakeの原料となるお米の精米歩合は、75％以下のものが多く用いられています。

酒造りで使われる「米を磨く」ということばは、まさにこの精米歩合のことを指すのです。はじめは大粒だったお米も、60％、50％と磨いていくうちに、どんどん小さく丸くなっていきます。こうした精米技術も、酒造りの重要な要素です。

イタリア産の米を原料としたアルコール飲料は出来るかもしれないけれど、日本酒を造ることはそんなに簡単ではないことを、どう伝えるべきか、私は大変悩んだのでした。

（参考：『日本酒百味百題』小泉武夫監修／柴田書店刊）

O-sake and Rice

"Can we make sake using our rice?" This is a question I was frequently asked by major Italian rice producers when I attended the Salone Del Gusto, a food festival in Trino, Italy, when I introduced Japanese sake there.

To produce sake, only a few kinds of rice are used, unlike rice served for meals. Strains of rice such as Yamada Nishiki, Gohyakumangoku, Miyama Nishiki, and Omachi, are used to produce o-sake.

The grain of these strains of rice is bigger in size, has a larger center-core, and less protein, than the strains of rice served for meals. If rice contains many minerals and vitamins and a high percentage of fat, the flavor, taste, and color of o-sake will be impaired.

To avoid this, rice grains are milled and polished until they transform into round shapes like pearls. It is not that easy to produce o-sake using Italian rice, considering the minute processes.

Having said that, I did not want to give the impression that the sake manufacturing processes, which are based on the Japanese *terroir*, have no equal. So, I searched my brain for an answer.

(Source: *Nihonshu Hyakumi Hyakudai*, Takeo Koizumi, Shibata Publishing Co. Ltd.)

枡のなかのお米は、酒造好適米を、50%に磨いたもの
The rice put in a masu is a type of rice approved to be suitable for sake brewing. It is polished by 50%.

Scene 3

It's Party Time!

Osakeとスイーツの
パーティーにようこそ!

パーティーの楽しさは、
家族や仲間たちとの会話はもちろんのこと、
舌や目を楽しませてくれる「意外性」や「驚き」がとても大切です。
Osakeとスイーツの組み合わせをマスターして、
テーブルコーディネートと共に、「素敵な驚き」を演出してみませんか。

One of the joys we experience at a party is conversation.
But, in addition to that, elements of surprise and
pleasure to the eye and tongue are vitally important.
Why don't you create a pleasant surprise?

フルーツのババロア　キル フェ ボン⑭／ミニカップ　玉有ⓒ
Bavaroise aux Fruits　Qu'il Fait Bon⑭／Mini Cup　Gyokuyuⓒ

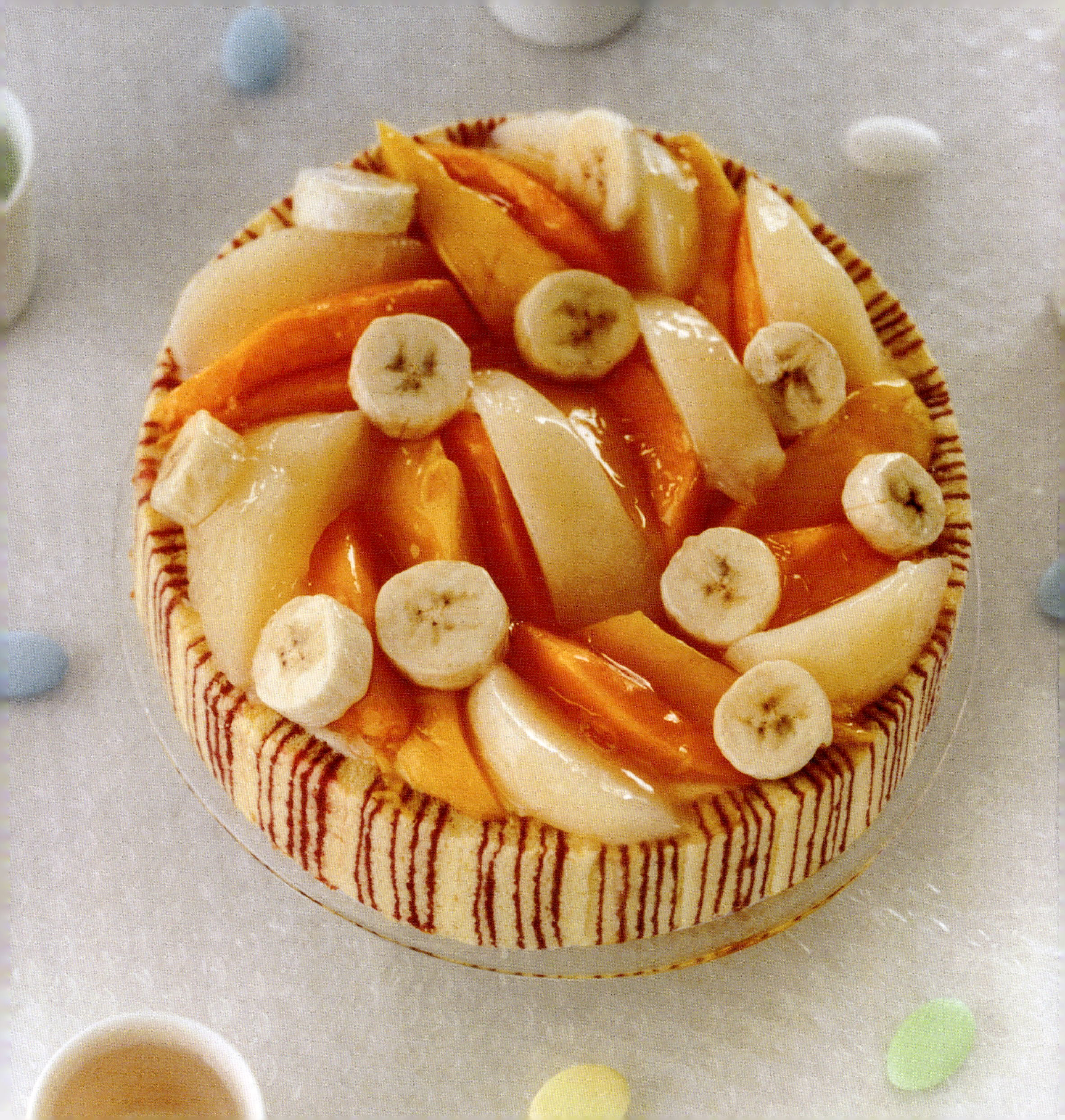

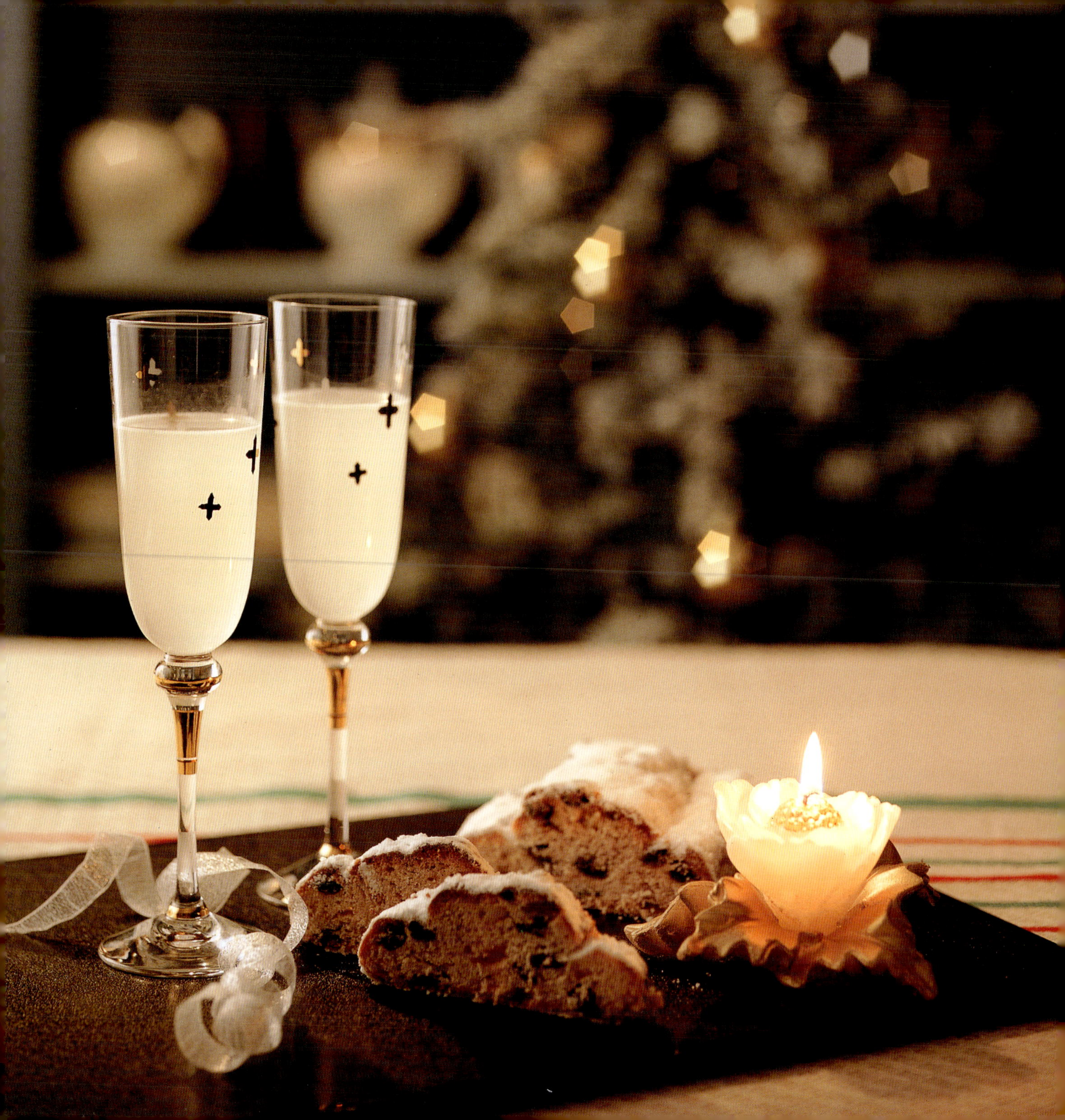

発泡酒とドイツのクリスマス菓子でイヴを祝う
純米大吟醸 FN(フォーミュラ・ニッポン) & シュトレン

イタリアでは、クリスマスにスプマンテ（発泡性ワイン）とパネトーネ（ドライフルーツなどが入った円筒形のパンケーキ）でお祝いをする習慣があります。フランスのシャンパーニュ、ドイツのゼクト、スペインのカヴァなど、スパークリングワインは、どこの国でもお祝いごとには欠かせませんが、スパークリングOsakeと Made in Japan のシュトレンで祝うクリスマスは、なかなか新鮮です。シュトレンのどっしりとした味わいが、キレ味のよいOsakeに包まれて、口のなかで華やかに溶け合います。

Junmai Dai-ginjo FN & Stollen

In Italy, they celebrate Christmas with *spumante* (sparkling wine) and *panettone*. Sparkling wines are essential on auspicious days; *champagne* in France, *sekt* in Germany, *cava* in Spain. To drink sparkling o-sake and eat stollen that is made in Japan is an interesting way to commemorate Christmas.

It's Party Time!
13
APHRODISIAC

漆のトレイ
黒という色は、食卓で使うには、とても難しいのですが、焼き菓子のような素朴な色合いのスイーツを盛りつけると、シックに引き立ちます。／黒乾漆ランチョン　ちきりや⑪

Lacquerware Tray
The color black is a difficult color to use in decorating a dining table. However, when you put a simple baked cake on a black plate, it serves as a perfect foil to create a chic ambience.／Black Lacquer Coating Luncheon Tray Chikiriya Inc.⑪

シュトレン
ドイツの伝統的なクリスマス菓子シュトレン。イヴの夜に向けて、薄く切って、少しづつ食べるのがドイツ流。噛むほどに深い味わいのある、素材にこだわった逸品。／パティシエ イナムラ ショウゾウ⑪

Stollen
This is a traditional German Christmas cake and is eaten in the week or so prior to Christmas Eve. The more you savor the cake, the more you will find a profound palate. This cake is made of choice ingredients.／P'ÂTISSIER INAMURA SHOZO⑪

純米大吟醸 FN (福島)
日本酒にはめずらしいドライな飲み口のスパークリングOsakeは、よく冷やして、極上の蕎麦を食べる前の一杯のアペリティフとしてもおすすめです。／奥の松酒造(P.95)

Junmai Dai-ginjo FN
This is a rare sparkling o-sake: it is dry. It is best chilled. This will serve as an aperitif to provide an appetizing background for a meal, especially when you consume good quality soba noodles.／OKUNOMATSU SAKE BREWERY CO., LTD. (P.95)

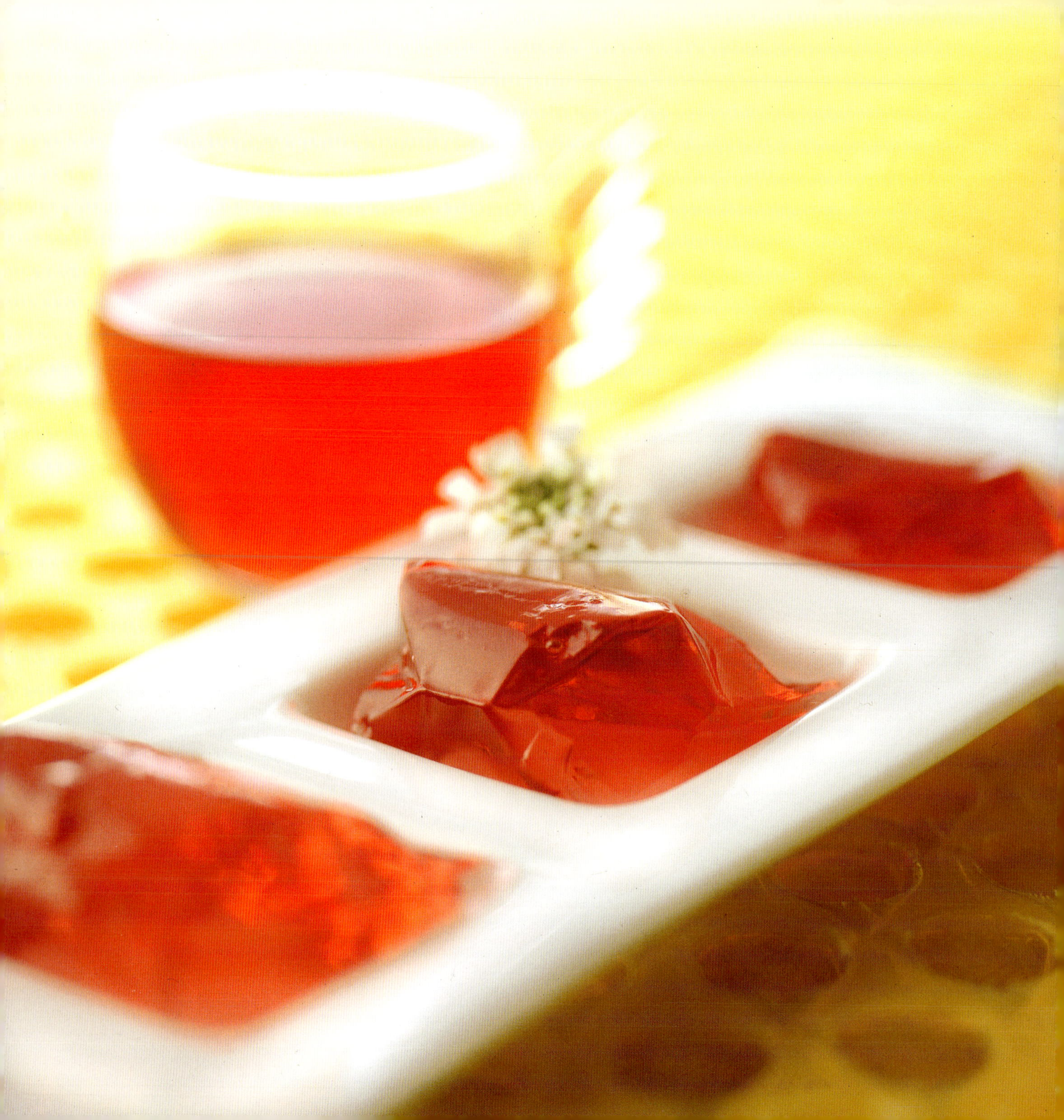

It's Party Time! 14

ルビー色のハーブカクテルで初夏を過ごす
Osake cocktail カンパーニュ＆梅エキスのゼリー

テーブルに敷いたプラスティックハニカム（内装材の一種）の黄色、カクテルとゼリーの赤。どれも透明感のある明るい色彩に、光沢のあるお皿の白を加えた、元気の出るカラーコーディネートです。Osakeの旨味に溶け込んだ、ローズヒップなどのハーブの甘酸っぱい風味が、蒸し暑い日本の夏に喜ばれる、さわやかなカクテル。梅の香りと控えめな甘さが、カクテルの味を引き立てます。「ルビー色のアクセサリーを身に付けてきてください」。こんなドレスコードが似合う初夏のパーティーです。

"Campagne" & Plum Essence Jelly
The honeycomb patterned plastic sheet and red color of the jelly make a bright contrast to the white lusterware. The sweet and sour taste of rosehip is an excellent partner for steamy summers like those in Japan. The subtle sweetness of plum lends an air of freshness.

長方形のお皿とグラス
まるでパレットのような白いお皿には、色とりどりのゼリーを盛り付けても楽しそう。取っ手に天使の羽をモチーフにしたグラスが、食卓のアクセントに。／スクエア3パレット　玉有©／グラス　エンジェルシリーズ　Sugahara®

Palette-shaped Plate and Glass
A colorful jelly on a palette-shaped dish creates a cheerful atmosphere. Angel wings attached to the glass give a playful accent to the table.／Oblong palette Gyokuyu©／Glass Angel Series　SUGAHARA GLASSWORKS, INC.®

手島麻記子のOsake cocktail
カンパーニュ
レシピ：720ml分
材料：低アルコールタイプの純米酒または純米酒720ml／ドライハーブ　ティースプーン3〜4杯（ハイビスカス、りんご、ローズヒップ、イチゴがブレンドされた、ウィッタードのフルーツティー「サマーストロベリー」を使っています。）
作り方：ガラスのピッチャーにOsakeとハーブを入れ、冷蔵庫で3〜4時間冷やすと、色も鮮やかな、香りのよいハーブカクテルが出来上がります。

梅エキスのゼリー
自社農園で育てた城州白梅といわれる品種を、樹の上で完熟させた後、自社貯蔵庫で3年間じっくり寝かせ、その梅エキスをゼリーとしたこだわりのスイーツ。／標野（しめの）　菓匠 叶匠壽庵⑫

Makiko Tejima's O-sake Cocktail "Campagne"
Recipe for 720ml:
Ingredients: Low alcohol or ordinary junmai-shu 720ml／Dried herbal tea leaves 3-4 tea spoons (Use the fruit tea made by Whitterd, "Summer Strawberry", mixed blend of hibiscus, apple, rosehip, and strawberry.)
How to prepare: Pour the bottle of o-sake into a pitcher and add the herbal tea leaves. Then, chill it in the refrigerator for 3-4 hours. You will find it a colorful and fragrant herb cocktail.

Plum Essence Jelly
The type of plum used for the jelly is the Joshu white plum. After the plums are fully ripened, they are stored for three years in refrigerators. The concentrated plum juice is used for this jelly.／KANO SHOJUAN⑫

チーズケーキ
heese Cake
mément à la tradition
PÂTISSERIE
OVER
vieilles provinces

It's Party Time! 15

懐かしい友人と過ごす素敵なひととき
すず音&
チーズケーキ

すっきりとした飲み口に伴われた、しっかりとした味わいのOsakeと、チーズケーキのコクが溶け合って、口のなかでナチュラルな甘さが広がります。かわいらしいパッケージに入ったケーキとOsakeを手土産に、懐かしい友人を訪ねて、ゆっくり過ごしてみませんか。計画して開くパーティーも楽しいけれど、不意の来客を受けての、気取りのないパーティーも素敵です。そして何よりも、思いたったときにふらりと訪ねていける友人がいる幸せと、それを喜んで受け入れられる関係が、Osakeを一層おいしくしてくれます。

Suzune & Cheesecake

The clear palate of this o-sake marries happily with the rich and substantial taste of this cheesecake. Why don't you put a cake in an attractive package and visit an old friend? It might be nice to drop in on someone you haven't seen in a while.

SEDATIVE

大きな平皿
日本の染め付けを思い起こさせる、ブルー一色で描かれたフランスの硬質陶器メーカーのお皿。直径30センチというサイズは、パーティートレイとしても便利。／ケークプラター（オアゾブルー）ジアン青山本店Ⓚ／グラス　日本の酒情報館SAKE PLAZAⒶ

Big Plate
This French ironstone china reminds me of Japanese blue-and-white ware. The diameter of the plate is 30 cm. It will do as a party tray./Cake platter (Oiseau Bleu) Gien Aoyama BoutiqueⓀ/Glass SAKE PLAZAⒶ

チーズケーキ
小ぶりなサイズですが、食べごたえはたっぷり。飾り気のない素朴な味わいが、後を引くおいしさです。人気商品のため、予約をおすすめします。スチームベークタイプ。／ふらんす菓子クローバー⑬

Cheesecake
Although this cake is small, it is filling. Its unpretentious and simple aftertaste is irresistible. Since this is a popular item, it is essential to order it in advance./PÂTISSERIE CLOVER⑬

すず音（宮城）
和風の名前からは想像できないほど、チーズとよく合います。特にフルーツの入ったクリームチーズは、Osakeの味を引き立てる絶妙なおつまみに。／一ノ蔵（P.94）

Suzune
This o-sake is goes unexpectedly well with cream cheese, especially ones containing fruit./Ichinokura Co., Ltd. (P.94)

049

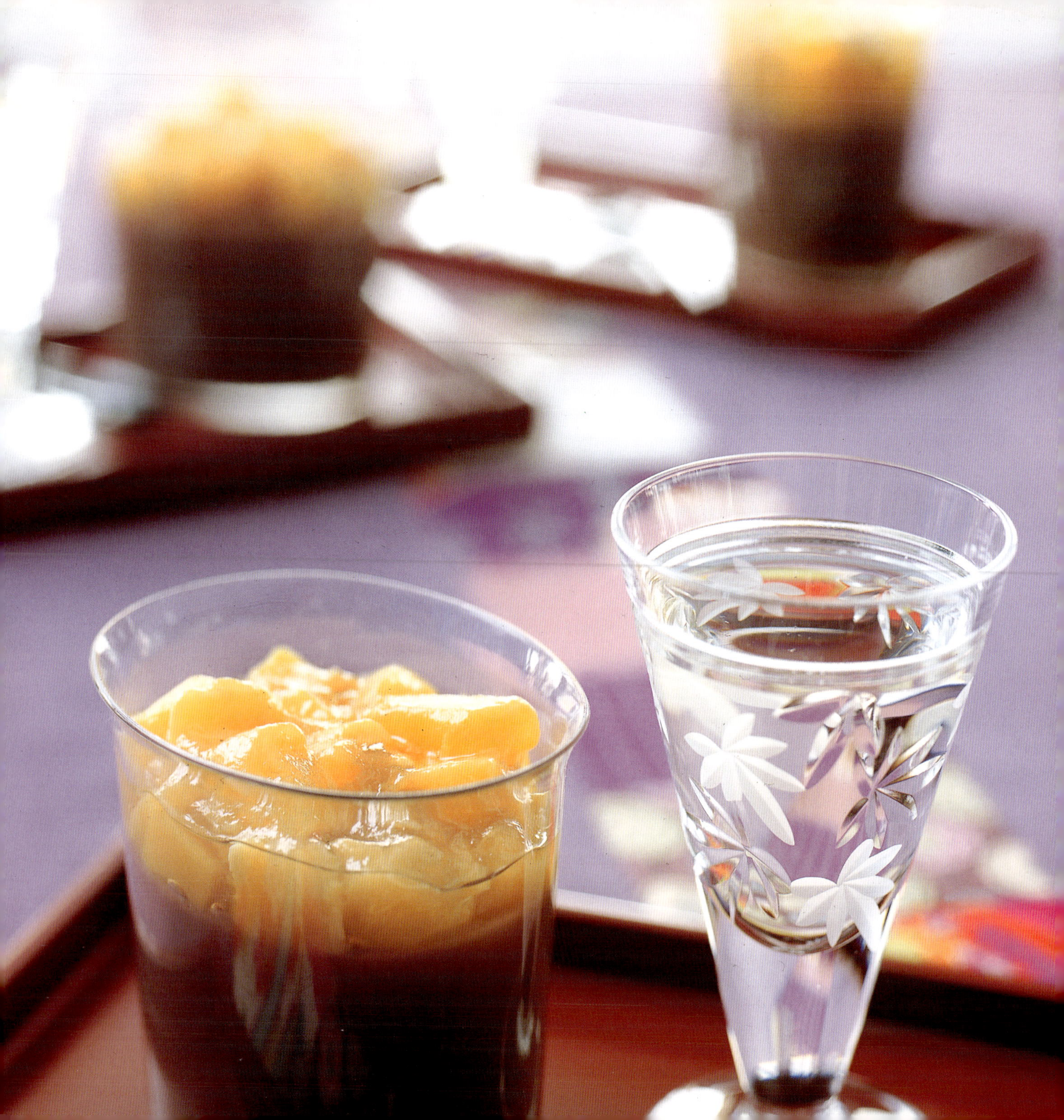

It's Party Time! 16

意外な取り合わせが、楽しい驚きをプレゼント
萩の白露 &
葛あずきとマンゴー

ほっと心なごむやさしい味わいのOsakeが、こしあんとマンゴーという意外な組み合わせのスイーツに出合うと、違った一面をのぞかせます。マンゴーの酸味とこしあんの甘みが、Osakeだけを飲んだときには表だってはいなかった、お米の旨味を充分に引き出します。寒天でもゼラチンでもない、葛の触感が、何とも新鮮で、楽しい驚きをプレゼントしてくれます。Osakeとあんこという、最も合わせにくいイメージの取り合わせも、こんな新しいセンスのスイーツの前では、すっかりイメージチェンジです。

Hagi no Shiratsuyu & Kuzu*¹ Azuki and Mango

When the soothing taste of this o-sake marries azuki, or strained red bean jam, and mango, they show a different aspect of their characters. The acidity of the mango and the sweetness of the jam double the exquisite taste of this o-sake. The texture of *kuzu* should give you a pleasant surprise. This combination of o-sake and jam is unexpectedly complementary.

朱色のお皿
紫のテーブルクロスと漆の朱色が、アジアンアンティックな雰囲気を演出します。小さめなサイズは、ひとり分のOsake&スイーツトレイとして、パーティーで大活躍です。／長角取皿　ちきりや⒣／冷酒グラス〈楓〉　HOYA（株）クリスタルカンパニー①

Vermillion Colored Plate
The purple tablecloth and cinnabar lacquerware create an Asian atmosphere. You can use the lacquerware as a tray when you serve o-sake and desserts at a party.／Oblong Small Plate　Chikiriya Inc.⒣／Glass for Cold Sake 〈Kaede (Maple)〉　HOYA CORPORATION Crystal Company①

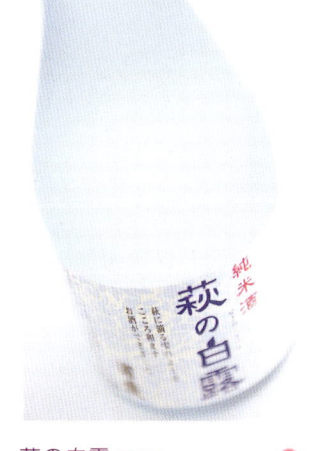

葛あずきとマンゴー
いちご大福をはじめて食べたときの驚きに匹敵する、意外なマッチングのおいしさ。また食べてみたくなる、スイーツの新しい和テイストです。／木風⑥

Kuzu*¹ Azuki and Mango
A better-than-expected marriage between red bean jam and mango equals strawberry *daifuku**² in taste.／KIKAZE.⑥ (*¹Kuzu: A member of a pulse family. Jelly is produced from the dried roots. *²Daifuku: a traditional Japanese dessert. Red bean jam is covered with rice cake.)

萩の白露（宮城）
酢豚のような甘酸っぱく、とろみのある料理のよきパートナーになってくれます。引き立て役が上手な、静かなOsakeです。／佐浦（P.93）

Hagi no Shiratsuyu (Dew of Hagi)
This o-sake matches dishes with a sweet and sour taste and thick texture like sweet and sour pork. The taste of this o-sake serves as an excellent foil for the dishes.／Saura Co., Ltd. (P.93)

STIMULANT

051

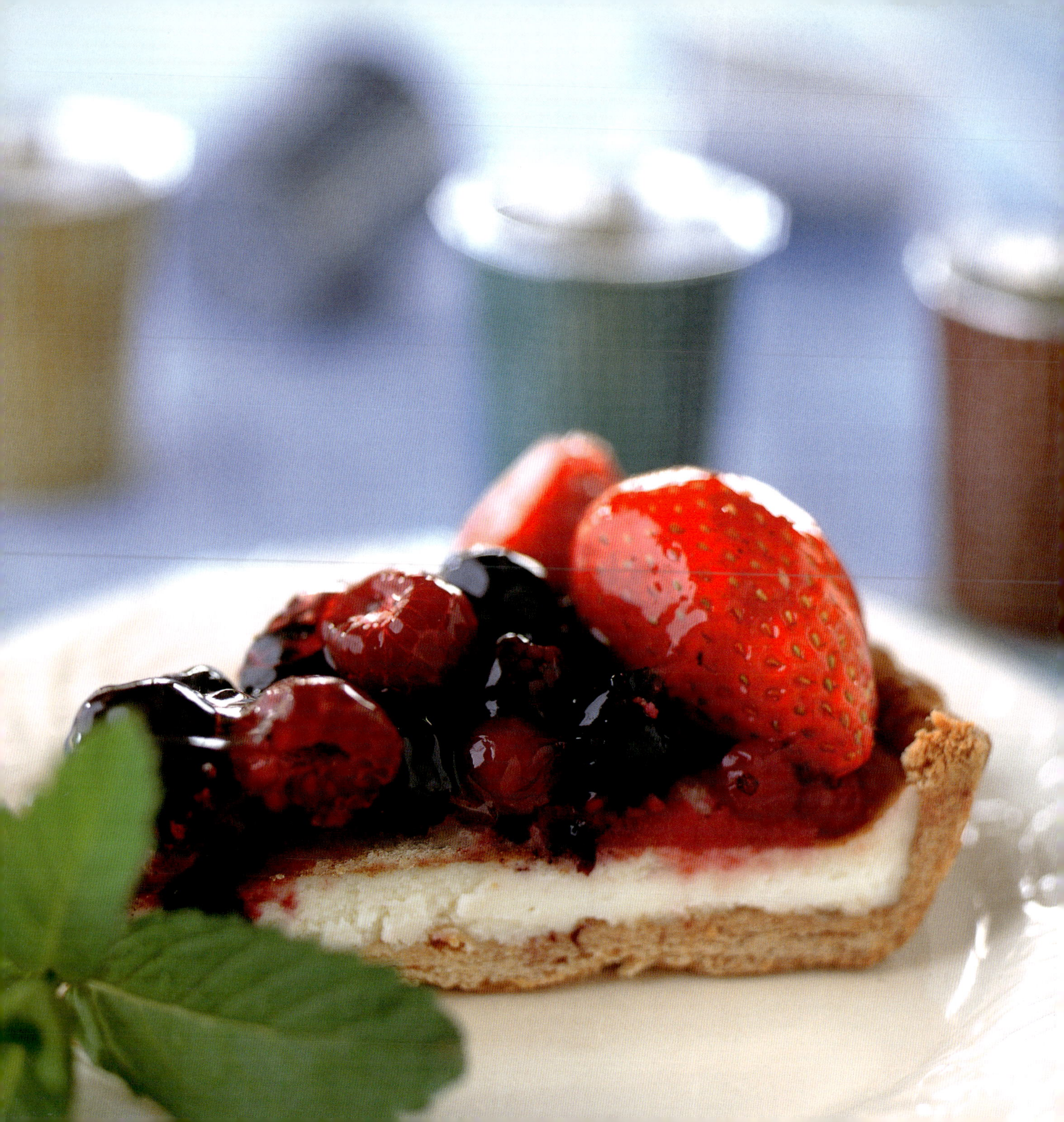

It's Party Time! 17

甘酸っぱさと淡い花の香りを、雅な雰囲気で
花かほり＆
フルーツタルト

いちご、ラズベリー、フランボワーズなど、赤い果実の実がたっぷりとのったタルト。その甘酸っぱさが、淡い花の香りを感じさせる、さらりとしたOsakeの風味と交じり合い、サクサクしたタルト生地と一緒に、口のなかでやさしく溶け合います。独特な光沢を放つ錫の表面に、摺漆(すりうるし)を施したカラフルなぐい呑みは、食卓に雅な雰囲気を演出します。女友達3人で、時には優雅な気分で、素敵な恋の話に花を咲かせてみませんか。

Hana Kaori & Fruit Tart

Tarts are covered with red berries such as strawberries and raspberries. The sweet and sour taste of the berries matches the acidic taste of this o-sake. The crispy tart texture and the jammy fruits harmonize in the palate. When poured into tin lacquer cups with a matte finish, o-sake emits a mellower taste. Why don't we talk about our love lives with female friends?

錫製のぐい呑み
錫は、熱伝導性が高いので、ぐい呑みを持った手のひらに、冷たくしたOsakeのひんやりとし感触が伝わってきます。／源氏物語みゆきシリーズ　大阪錫器Ⓔ

Tin Guinomi Cup
When you put this cup in your hand, you can feel its cool temperature./The Tale of Genji Royal Visit Series Osaka Suzuki Co., Ltd.Ⓔ

フルーツタルト
季節の新鮮なフルーツをふんだんに使ったタルトといえばここ。ついつい食べ過ぎてしまう、自然な甘さです。／赤いフルーツのタルト　キル フェ ボン⑭

Fruit Tart
If you look for tarts filled with abundant fresh fruits, buy them at Qu'il Fait Bon. It is hard to stop eating them. They have a natural sweet taste./Qu'il fait bon⑭

花かほり（山口）
山口県産の桜酵母を使って造った純米吟醸酒。飲んだ後に、口のなかで広がる華やかな香りが、フルーツと良く合います。／山縣本店（P.100）

Hana no Kaori（Scent of Flowers）
This junmai-ginjo-shu is made using cherry blossom yeast from Yamaguchi Prefecture. The lingering flowery scent of the o-sake goes well with fruit. /Yamagata Honten (P.100)

EUPHORIC

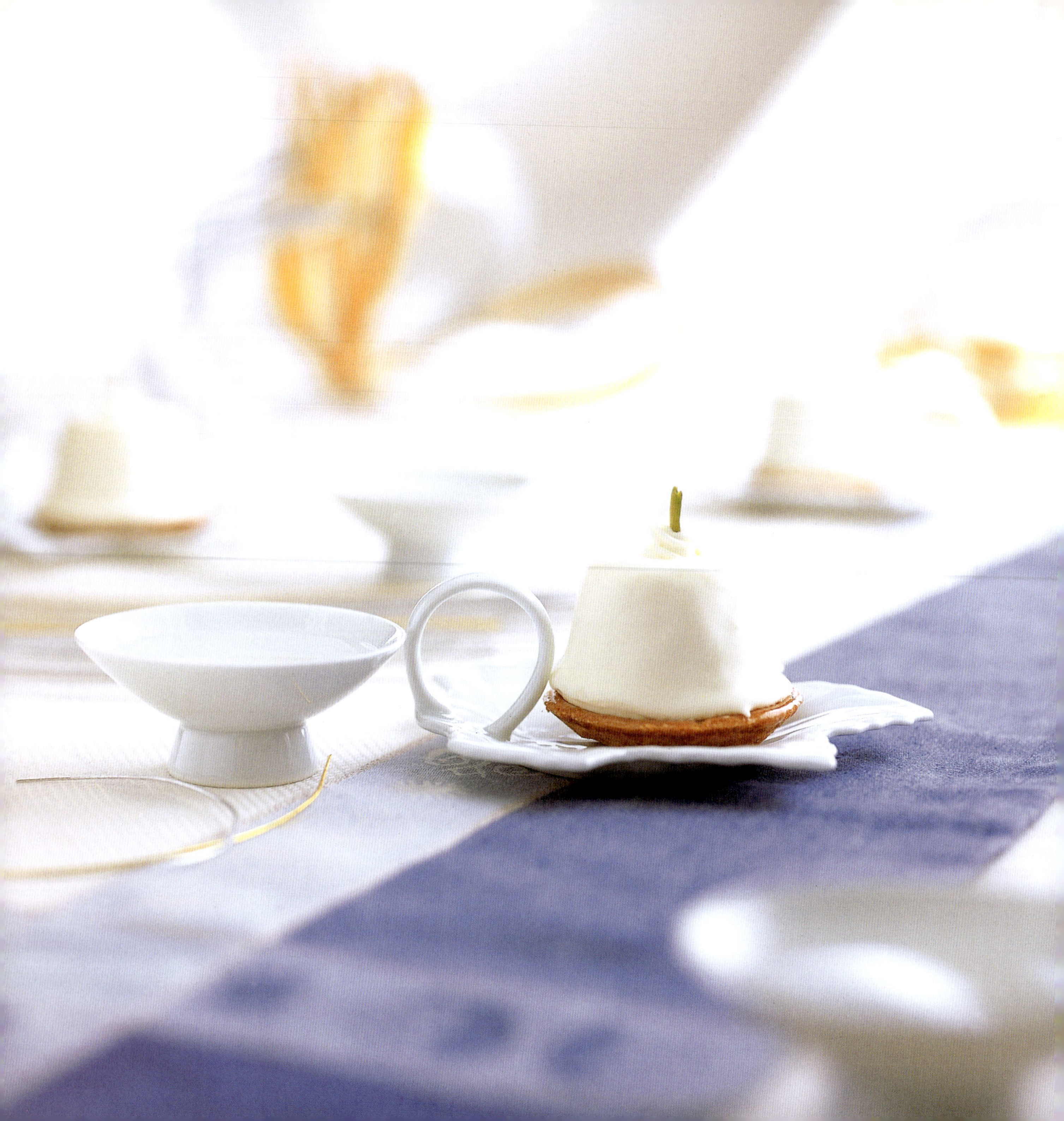

It's Party Time!

18

純白のスイーツと辛口酒で祝うNew Year
上撰松竹梅 超淡麗辛口「生冷酒」焙炒造り&
レアチーズケーキ

大晦日の夜のカウントダウンパーティーを、新しい年にふさわしいまっ白なスイーツと、気分も引き締まるようなキリッとした味わいのOsakeで祝ってみませんか。独特の香りを放つ、口あたりのなめらかな辛口のOsakeが、レアチーズケーキのクリーミーな味わいを引き立てます。リーフ型のお皿の立体的な取っ手のデザインに合わせ、テーブルの奥に水引をあしらってみました。オリジナリティ溢れるスイーツの形も楽しい味わいのひとつです。

Josen Sho-chiku-bai Chou Tanrei Karakuchi "Raw cold sake" Roasting Method & Rare Cheesecake

When you celebrate New Year's Eve, why don't you consume an impeccably white dessert with this brisk tasting o-sake? The distinctive flavor and dry taste of this o-sake enriches the creamy cheesecake. I placed the cake on a leaf-shaped plate and used a tablecloth with *mizuhiki* ribbons, an auspicious Japanese motif. Original presentation is one of the pleasures of enjoying desserts.

シュガーリーフトレイ
ティータイムに角砂糖などをのせて使うので、他の人にも回しやすいように取っ手がついています。小さなスイーツをのせてケーキ皿にも。／盃共に、玉有 ©

Sugar Leaf Tray
This is used for sugar cubes at teatime. You can also use it as a plate to serve small desserts./Tray and Sake Cup Gyokuyu ©

レアチーズケーキ
濃厚なチーズのコクと、フレッシュな生クリームが溶け合った、素材の持ち味が凝縮された、スイーツ。／フロマージュ クリュ オーボンヴュータン ⑮

Rare Cheesecake
The rich taste of the cheese and the fresh whipped cream are mixed. A concentrated excellent taste is realized in this dessert, making the most of the characteristics of the ingredients./Fromage Crue Au Bon Vieux Temps ⑮

上撰松竹梅 超淡麗辛口「生冷酒」焙炒造り（京都）▲
個性的な香りと、はっきりとしたストレートな味わいは、ローズマリーを使ったラムの香草焼きなどとよく合います。／宝酒造 (P.99)

Josen Sho-chiku-bai Chou Tanrei Karakuchi "Raw cold sake" Roasting Method
The unique flavor of this o-sake marries well with roast lamb and rosemary./Takara Shuzo Co., Ltd. (P.99)

REGULATING

055

Hot Osakeの楽しみ方

　日向燗(約30℃)、人肌燗(約35℃)、ぬる燗(約40℃)、上燗(約45℃)、熱燗(約50℃)、飛び切り燗(55℃、またはそれ以上)。Osakeの燗の付け方に、温度の違いによるこれほどのバラエティがあることを知ったときは、驚きでした。

　明治時代を代表する教育者のひとりである福沢諭吉先生は、行灯の灯りのもとで深夜研究に励まれているときに、徳利を括り付け、行灯の熱で暖まったOsakeを飲むのを楽しみにしていたといいます。「行灯燗」と呼ばれたこのOsakeは、一体どんなぬくもりのOsakeだったのか、大変興味が湧きます。

　今や電子レンジで簡単にできる燗酒ですが、やはり湯煎で付けるOsakeは、ひと手間かける分だけ、徳利の上下で極端に温度差が出来ることもなく、何よりOsakeの風味がまろやかに引き立ちます。最近では徳利がない家も多いので、右上の写真にあるような燗付け器の「タンポ」(湯たんぽに由来することばともいわれている)も、家庭ではほとんど目にしなくなっています。

　お湯を張ったお鍋にOsakeの入った「タンポ」を入れて、頃合を見計らって引き上げる。Osakeの種類や季節によっても違う、そのタイミングが分かるようになったら、かなりのOsake通です。銅、アルミなど色々な種類がありますが、私はこの錫製の「タンポ」で付けた、角のとれたまあるいやさしい味が大好きです。

How to Enjoy Hot O-sake

When I learned that there are many temperatures for serving o-sake warm, I was very surprised. They are *Hinatakan* (literally, in the sun, about 30°C or 86°F), *Hitohadakan* (skin temperature, about 35°C or 95°F), *Nuru-kan* (lukewarm, about 40°C or 104°F), *Joukan* (warm, about 45°C or 113°F), *Atsukan* (hot, about 50°C or 122°F), and *Tobikirikan* (very hot, 55°C or over 131°F).

I also heard of another; *Andon* (oil lamp)-*Kan*. Yukichi Fukuzawa, one of the educators in Japan during the Meiji period (1868-1912) used to attach a sake container to a lamp while studying until late at night. He enjoyed drinking this hot o-sake. I wonder how hot it was and how it tasted.

Nowadays, it is quite easy to warm o-sake using a microwave. The best method is still the old-fashioned one of warming a tokkuri or a tampo, a small pitcher, in a pot of hot water. There may not be so many families who have a tampo. The word tampo appears to have been originated from *yutampo*, a hot-water bottle, or foot warmer. I prefer tampo made of tin, to copper or aluminum (see photo).

Put the tampo (or a tokkuri) in a pot of hot water and keep it at a steady temperature, just below simmering, so that the o-sake warms gradually. How it should be served on a particular occasion will depend on the setting, the season, the cuisine, the type and quality of the o-sake itself. By the time you acquire this skill, you will be a connoisseur of o-sake.

タンポ(燗付け器)1合、1.5合　大阪錫器Ⓔ
Tampo (Large: about 270cm³, Small: about 180cm³)　Osaka Suzuki Co., Ltd.Ⓔ

Scene 4
An Afternoon with O-sake

Osakeでアフタヌーン

午後のお茶の時間に楽しむOsakeは、もうそれだけでとても贅沢な気分。
飲み過ぎないように、スイーツと共に、ゆっくり味わいましょう。
まるで、コーヒーや紅茶を飲んでいるかのように、
漆のカップ&ソーサーにOsakeとスイーツをあしらって。
ほろ酔い気分で過ごす、夕方までの夢時間。ほんのりと紅くなった頬が、
食卓を囲む女性の美しさを引き立てます。

Drinking o-sake during afternoon tea time
makes us feel gorgeous.
Relish o-sake slowly with desserts.
Pour o-sake into lacquerware and
drink as if you are having coffee or tea with desserts.
The slight glow on your face will flatter your beauty.

マカロン ラトリエ ドゥ ジョエル・ロブション⑯／漆のカップ&ソーサー ちきりや㋪
Macaroon L'ATLIER De Joël Robuchon⑯／Lacquerware Cup and Saucer Chikiriya Inc.㋪

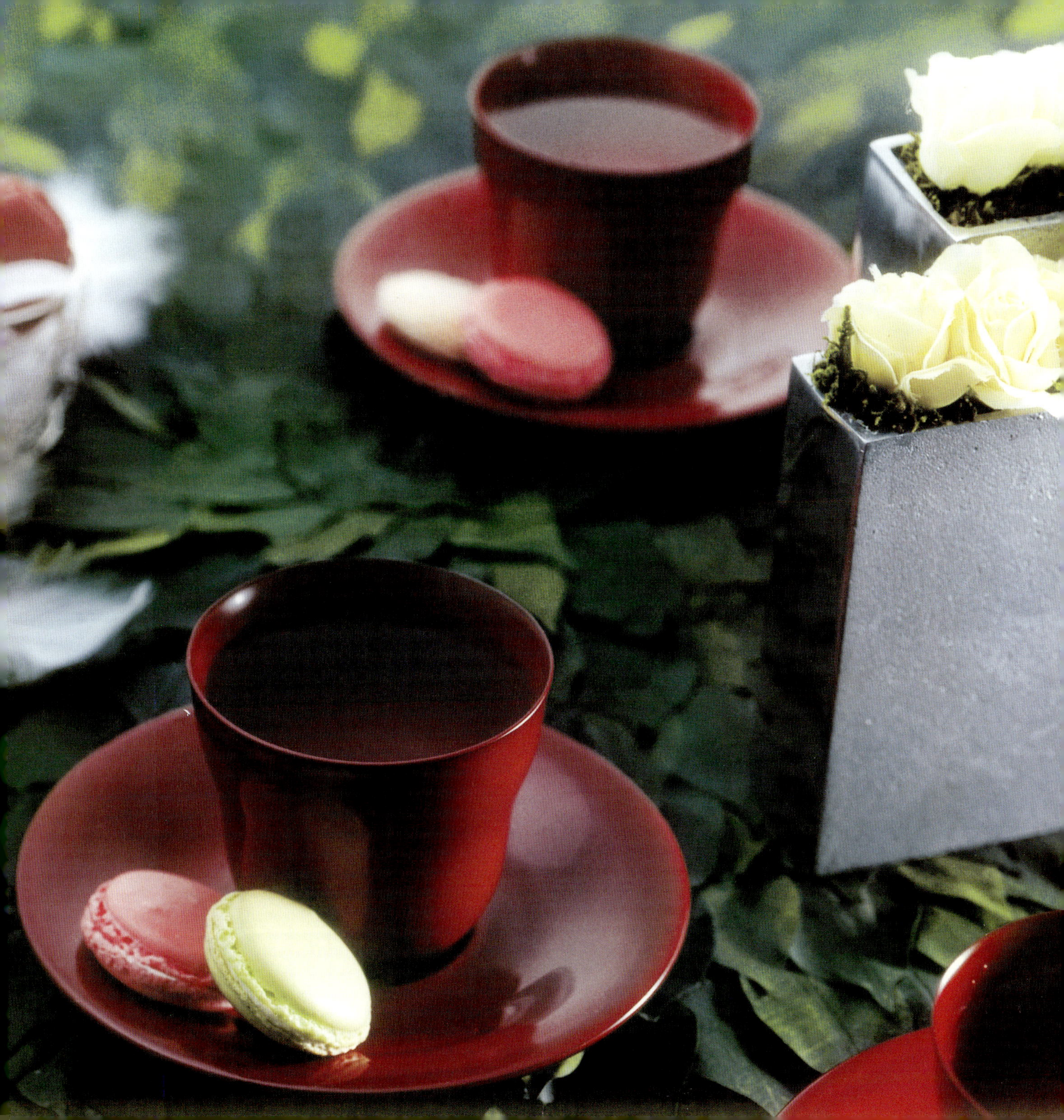

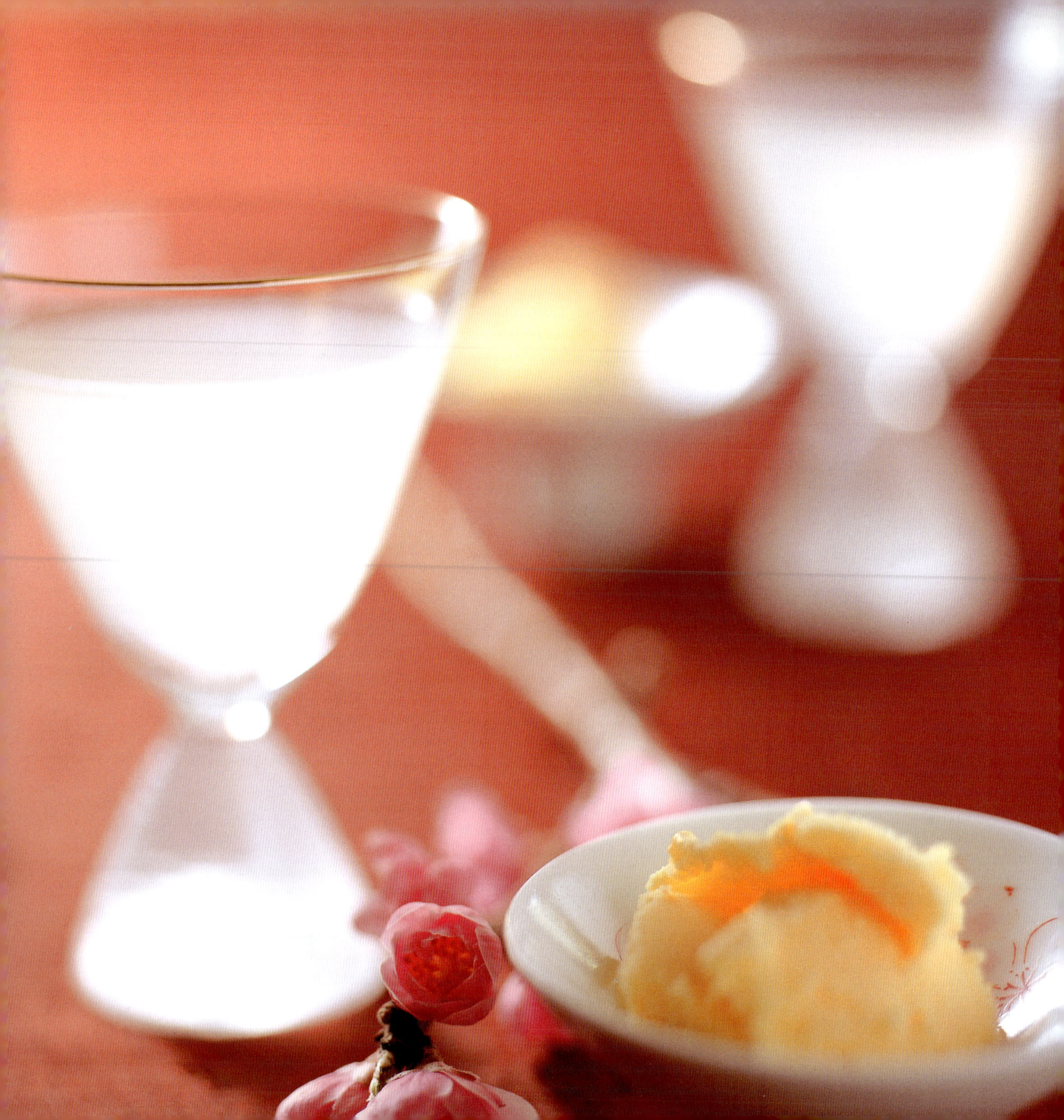

クールダウンしたい午後のひとときに
スイートハート&
マンゴーシャーベット

An Afternoon with O-sake
19

さわやかな口あたりのあとに、ゆっくりと広がるOsakeの甘さが、マンゴー独特の酸味とよく合い、カクテルを飲んでいるかのように、口のなかで見事に溶け合います。レシピによってさまざまですが、果物として食べる、熟れたマンゴーのねっとりとした触感を生かしたシャーベットとは、抜群の相性です。情熱的なカップルが、その溢れるばかりの熱い思いを、少し落ち着いて、クールダウンさせたい午後のひとときにおすすめです。

"Sweet Heart" & Mango Sorbet
The fresh, palatable, and sweet taste of this o-sake is complementary with the sour taste of mango. The moist texture of mango remains intact in the sorbet. It is a perfect match. This dessert is ideal for when a couple wants to cool down.

小皿として使うお猪口
シャーベットを盛り付けたのは、白磁にピンクのさくら模様が美しいお猪口。数回に分けて、スプーンで山高になるように盛り付けます。／盃 舞桜 玉有Ⓒ／冷酒杯 HOYA (株) クリスタルカンパニー①

Small Sake Cup
Sorbet is placed in a small sake cup with floating pink cherry blossom patterns painted on white porcelain. ／Sake Cup Mai-zakura Gyokuyu Ⓒ／Cup for Cold Sake HOYA CORPORATION Crystal Company ①

マンゴーシャーベット
トロピカルフルーツの代表的なマンゴーは、豊富なビタミンAと、たった1個で1日に必要なビタミンCの半分以上を摂取できるという優れものです。

Mango Sorbet
Mango is a representative tropical fruit which is rich in vitamins. If you eat one mango, you can get half of your daily vitamin C requirement. Very healthy!

スイートハート（神奈川）
料理に合わせるというよりは、素材そのものと合わせることで、互いを引き立て合う自然な甘さの微発泡酒です。／井上酒造 (P.98)

"Sweet Heart"
This o-sake should be not chosen by the cuisine but by the ingredients of a dish. It will make a harmony between the o-sake and basic dishes. This is a sparkling sake with natural sweetness. ／INOUYE BREWING CO., LTD. (P.98)

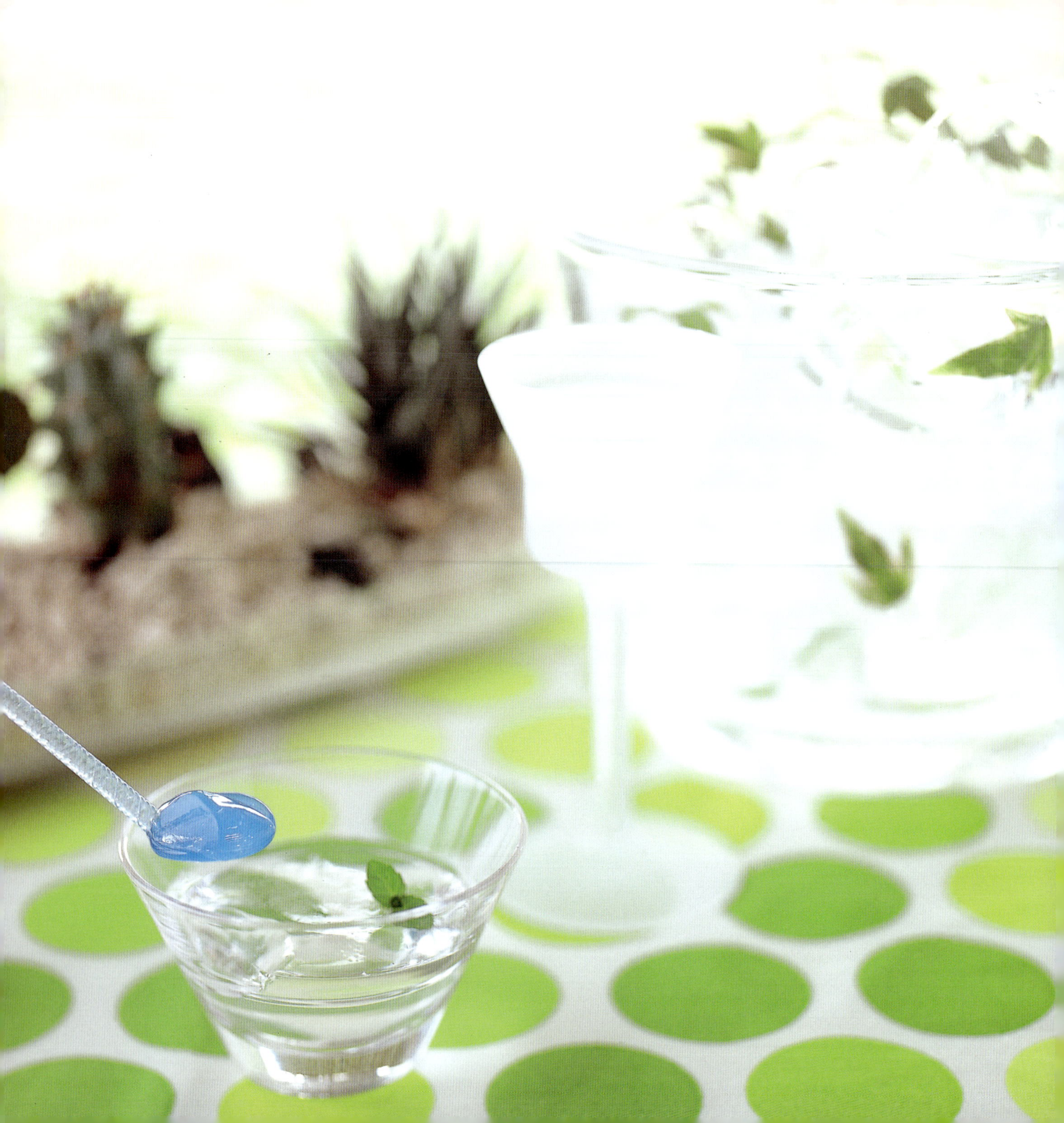

陽射し強い夏の午後の、爽快なティータイム

吟醸 上善如水 &
水のゼリー（夏みかんリキュール入り）

強い陽射しが差し込む夏の午後、キリッと冷したOsakeと手作りキットで作る水のゼリーはいかがですか。Osakeを造るときに使われる水は、仕込み水といわれ、その土地ごとに違います。涌き出る石清水や地下水など、自然の恵みがたっぷり含まれた仕込み水は、Osakeの味をつくり出す大切な原料です。この仕込み水を使ってゼリーを作ってみました。萩の夏みかんを丸ごと絞り込んだリキュールを加えた、Osakeの香りのする透明な「仕込み水ゼリー」です。すっきりとした吟醸酒の香りに、夏みかんの甘酸っぱさが加わり、さわやかな夏のティータイムの始まりです。

Ginjo Jozen Mizu no Gotoshi & Water Jelly (with Summer Orange Liqueur)

How about consuming water jelly and chilled o-sake, feeling the strong sunshine, in the afternoon on a summer day? To produce this o-sake, they use spring water, full of the blessings bestowed by nature. With this *Shikomi Sui**, I made jelly, adding orange liqueur. The light bouquet is accompanied by the refreshing taste of orange. This is a prelude to a fresh summer tea time.

フロストガラスのグラス
霜（フロスト）に被われたかのようなグラスで飲むOsakeは、その冷えた味わいを一層楽しめます。氷をいれたクーラーにはアイビーの葉をあしらって涼しげに。／フロストグラス、小鉢、トックリ、ボトルクーラー、すべてSugahara⑧

Frosted Glass Ware
Drinking o-sake in a frosted glass will enhance the cool taste. Put some ivy leaves in the wine cooler./Frosted Glass Goblet, Small Glass Bowl, Tokkuri, and Wine Cooler SUGAHARA GLASSWORKS INC. ⑧

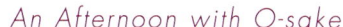

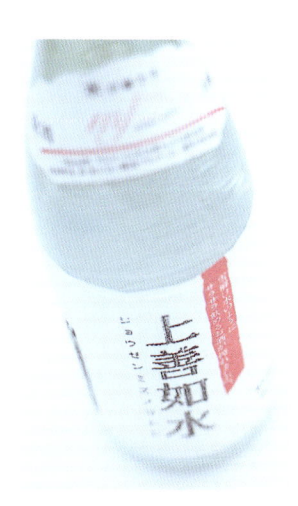

An Afternoon with O-sake
20

水のゼリー
パウダー状のゼリーの素に、カップまでついた手作りキット。旅先から持ち帰ったお水で、その土地の味を思い出しながら作るのも一興です。／水のゼリーの素　スイートランド・ナチュラルスイーツ⑰

夏みかんリキュール
山口県の清酒メーカーが造る、夏みかんを丸ごと使った米焼酎のリキュール。／夏みかんのかほり　山縣本店⑱

Water Jelly
If you use water you got during your trip reminiscing about the local cuisines, it will double your delight./A kit for making jelly Sweetland Co., Ltd. ⑰

Summer Orange Liqueur
Liqueur made of rice *shochu*. Produced by a sake brewer in Yamaguchi Prefecture, using whole summer oranges. /Yamagata Honten ⑱

吟醸 上善如水（新潟）
雪解け水のようにサラサラ飲めるOsakeの仕込み水は、地元湯沢の地下水。素材を生かしたシンプルな料理の味を引き立てます。／白瀧酒造（P.96）

Ginjo Jozen Mizu no Gotoshi
Light on the palate, it goes down quickly like melt water. The water (Shikomi Sui*) used to make this o-sake is local mineral water. It is excellent with simple cuisine. /SHIRATAKI SAKE BREWERY CO., LTD. (P.96) *Shikomi Sui: Water for brewing, more specifically, water used for fermentation. The pure water used is spring water or well water. Many brewers boast about their regions' "meisui" (famous water).

INVIGORATING

063

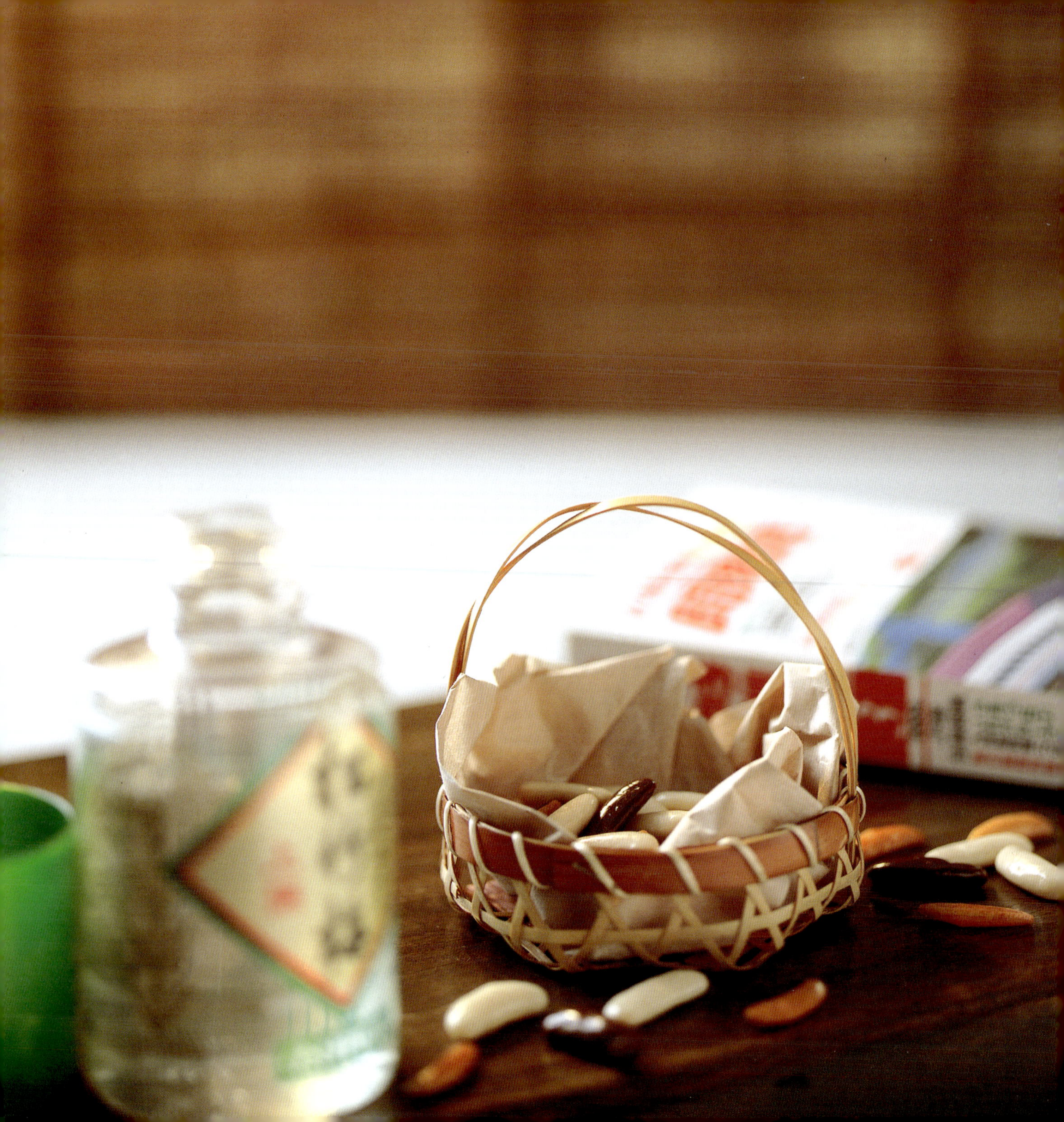

An Afternoon with O-sake

21

ゆったり旅気分にひたる午後のひととき
上撰 松竹梅「たけ」&
柿チョコ、ホワイト柿チョコ、柿の種

ふらりと旅に出かけたい、そんな思いで時刻表をながめるとき、こんなOsakeとおつまみがあったなら、気分はすでに車中の人。柿の種がOsakeに合うのは当たり前だけれども、チョコレートコーティングされた柿チョコが、辛口のOsakeをまろやかな風味に包み込みます。カリボリ、カリボリ、ブラックとホワイトを交互につまんでいると、ピリっとした柿の種も欲しくなり、甘辛3種類をお供に、ゆったりひとり旅気分は盛りあがります。縁側の日溜りで、うたた寝でもしたい午後のひとときです。

Josen Sho-Chiku-Bai (pine, bamboo, plum blossom) "Take" &
Persimmon Seed-shaped Snacks

You feel like traveling and you are looking at train schedules. If you have nibbles and drinks, you can use your imagination to take a trip. There are orange colored and persimmon seed-shaped salty rice snacks and snacks coated with black or white chocolate. This is well matched by dry o-sake. You might want to take a nap on the veranda this afternoon.

プラスチック蓋のカップ
ペットボトルタイプのこのOsakeは、蓋がそのまま器に。まるで、懐かしい水筒のカップで飲むような感覚のOsakeで、気分もなごみます。

Plastic Cup
The lid of the bottle of this sake can be used as a cup. This bottle evokes nostalgia in me and makes me feel warm and relaxed.

SEDATIVE

柿チョコ、ホワイト柿チョコ、柿の種
ミルキーな甘さのホワイトチョコの「ホワイト柿チョコ」が、このOsakeには特によく合います。柿チョコ、ホワイト柿チョコは、10月〜翌年3月末までの期間限定品。／浪花屋製菓⑲

Persimmon Seed-shaped Snacks
Black chocolate, white chocolate, and a salty taste are available. The milky sweet taste of this snack matches very well with this o-sake. ／NANIWAYASEIKA CO., LTD. ⑲

上撰松竹梅「たけ」(京都) ▲
河原で、釣った鮎の塩焼きと一緒に飲んだら最高！とイメージしたくなる、アウトドア派のOsakeです。／宝酒造（P.99）

Josen Sho-Chiku-Bai "Take"
It is terrific with sauted sweetfish (broiled with salt), especially when you caught them yourself.／Takara Shuzo Co., Ltd. (P.99)

065

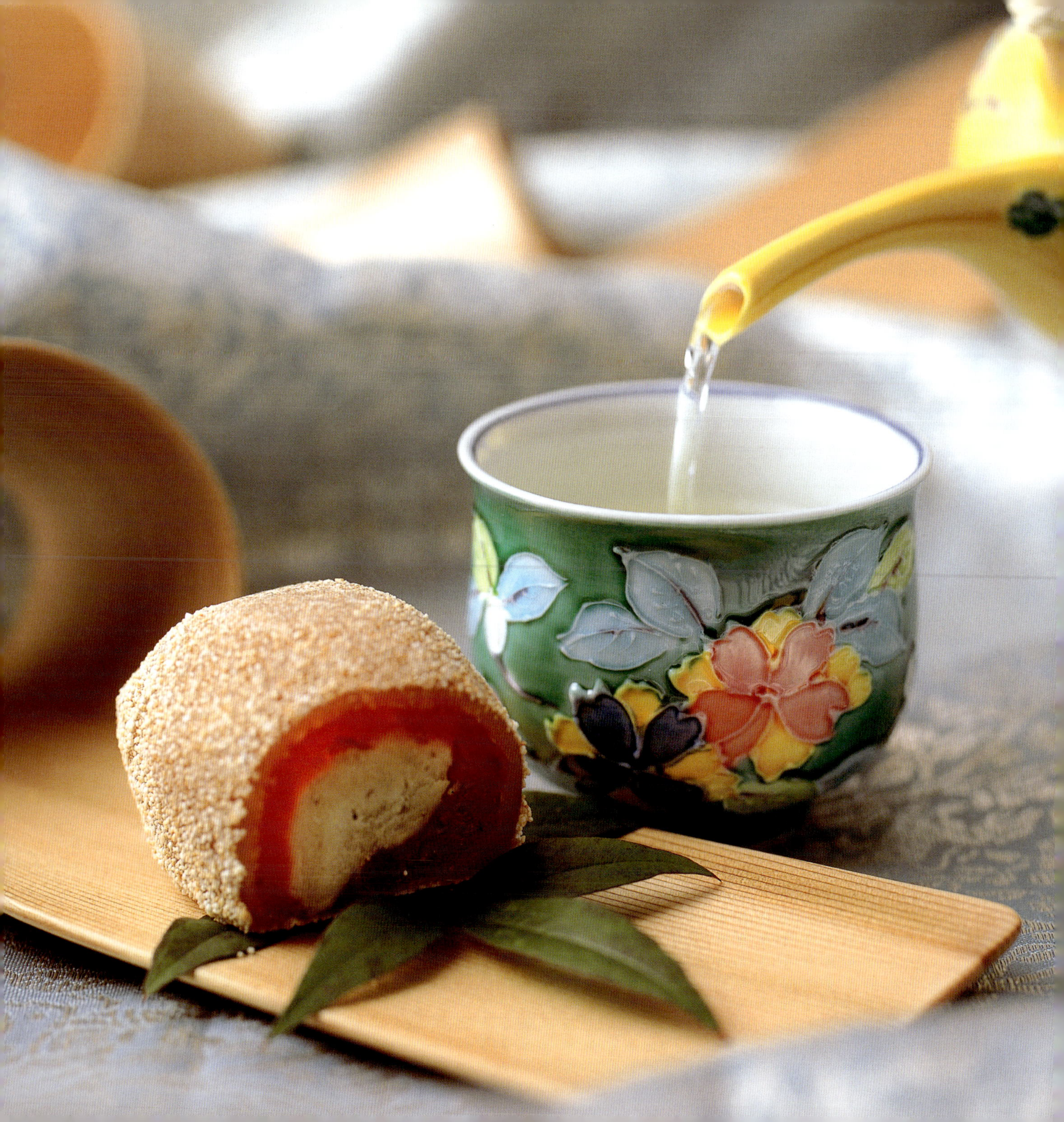

An Afternoon with O-sake

22

秋の陽射し、木の香り、ノスタルジックな午後
木桶仕込純米酒＆
栗きんとん入り干し柿

昔ながらの木桶で仕込んだ、しっかりとした味のOsakeが、秋の陽射しの元でじっくりと甘味を凝縮させた干し柿と栗きんとんの和菓子に出合い、やわらかな味わいとなって口のなかに広がります。Osakeから立ち昇るほのかな木の香りが、自然の恵みを上手に生かしながら生活を営んでいた、古き良き時代の日本を彷彿させ、ノスタルジックな気分に誘われます。酒器に描かれた花鳥風月を愛でる日本人の感性が、食卓に彩りを添え、午後の華やかなひとときを演出します。

Kioke Jikomi Junmai-shu & Mashed Chestnuts Covered with Dried Persimmon

This o-sake is made in the traditional method, using wooden casks. The distinctive taste of this o-sake marries nicely to this sweet Japanese cake, made of dried persimmons and chestnuts. The subtle flavor of the wood reminds me of the good old days of Japan. The flower patterns accent the table.

STIMULANT

清水焼きのぐい呑み
色鮮やかな黄色や緑、青で彩られた、交趾（こうち）と呼ばれている釉薬（ゆうやく）を使った酒器は、京都の焼き物らしい、ハレの食卓を演出するにふさわしい華やかさです。／青交趾さくらぐい呑み、黄交趾チロリ 洸春陶苑（こうしゅんとうえん）[L]／おしゃれ小皿 栗久[M]

Kiyomizu Ware Guinomi-style Cup
The vivid color contrast of this Kouchi glazed cup looks very Kyoto. It graces the table on special occasions.／Blue Kouchi Glazed Guinomi-style Cup and Yellow Kouchi-chirori Kousyun Touen[L]／Plate Kurikyu[M]

栗きんとん入り干し柿
信州市田の干し柿で栗きんとんを包み込んだ、上品な味ながら、良質な素材の味をたっぷりと堪能出来る逸品です。／久里柿 松月堂[20]

Mashed Chestnuts Covered with Dried Persimmon
This persimmon comes from Nagano Prefecture. Mashed chestnuts are covered with a dried persimmon. You can enjoy the bliss of nature.／Kuri Gaki Shogetsudo Co., Ltd.[20]

木桶仕込純米酒（福島）
木桶仕込みならではの、力強い味わいと独特な香りは、鴨のコンフィなどのしっかりとした肉料理にも合います。／奥の松酒造（P.95）

Kioke Jikomi Junmai-shu
It has a strong taste and a distinctive flavor with the characteristic nose of sake made with wooden casks. Excellent with meat dishes like duck confit.／OKUNOMATSU SAKE BREWERY CO., LTD. (P.95)

067

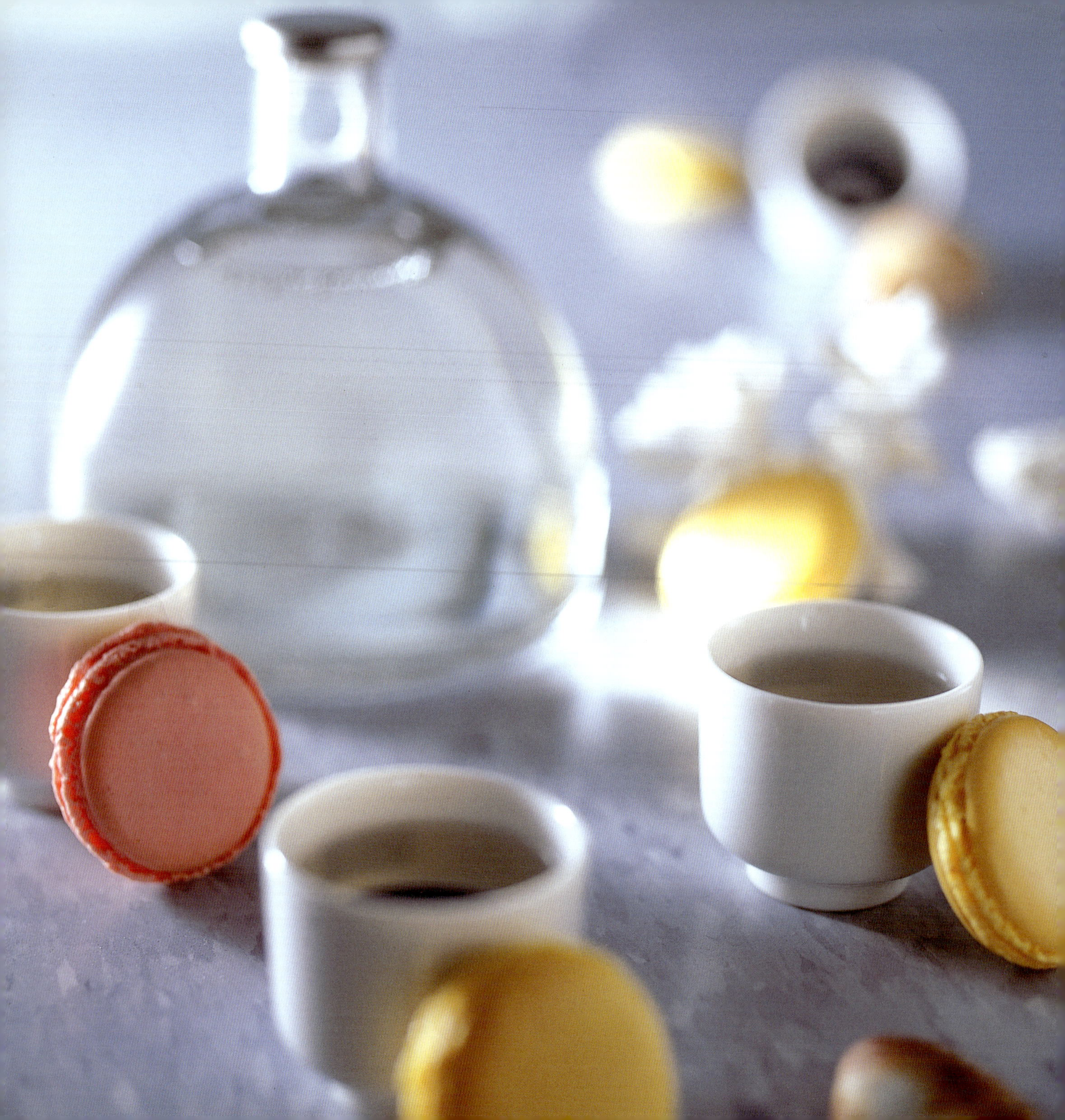

An Afternoon with O-sake

23

パリの定番スイーツと和の酒が醸す贅沢な時間
大吟醸ライト 水の王 &
レモン風味のマカロン

水のなかでゆらゆらと、魚たちと戯れながらOsakeが飲めたら…。こんなことを夢見たのは、グラスボードに乗って、宮古島の海中に潜ったことがきっかけです。透明感に満ちた味わいのOsakeと、フレッシュな風味が贅沢に凝縮されているマカロンとのティータイムは、心が洗われるような清雅な気分にしてくれます。パリのサロン・ド・テでは、定番のマカロン。本場パリでも、マカロンをOsakeと楽しむ日も近いのでは、と思わせるほどの相性です。

Miz no Eau &
Lemon Flavored Macaroon

I wish I could play with fish in the sea, wandering and drinking o-sake... I thought of this when I enjoyed diving in Miyako Island in Okinawa. The clear taste of o-sake and the fresh taste of macaroon should refresh our minds. At the *salons de thé* in Paris, macaroons are a staple. A superb marriage! The day may come where Parisiennes consume macaroons with o-sake.

きき猪口（ちょく）
きき酒用（200ml）に使われる、底に藍色の蛇の目模様を入れた白磁製の猪口のミニサイズ。Osakeの透明度がよく分かります。／日本の酒情報館 SAKE PLAZA Ⓐ

Kiki Choku (Cup for tasting)
The standard kiki choku is a white porcelain cup (200ml) with snake patterns on the bottom. You can realize the transparency of o-sake. The kiki choku in the photograph are much smaller than the regular size. ／SAKE PLAZA Ⓐ

レモン風味のマカロン
ロブションならではのこだわりの味が、レモンのほかに、チョコレート、コーヒー、ピスタチオ、フランボワーズとバラなど8種類楽しめる。／マカロンのシトロン（レモン）ラトリエ ドゥ ジョエル・ロブション ⑯

Lemon Flavored Macaroon
Since Robuchon is fastidious about palate, not only lemon but also chocolate, coffee, pistachio, strawberry, and rose flavors are available.／Macaroon (Lemon flavored) L'ATLIER De Joël Robuchon ⑯

大吟醸ライト 水の王（岩手）
今までの日本酒イメージからは想像も出来ない、流線型の透明ボトルに入ったOsake。素材を生かした、繊細な味の料理によく合います。／あさ開（P.92）

Miz no Eau
This is an unprecedented image for Japanese sake, using a transparent streamlined and simple bottle. Excellent with delicate and simple cuisines. ／Asabiraki Co., Ltd. (P.92)

EUPHORIC

069

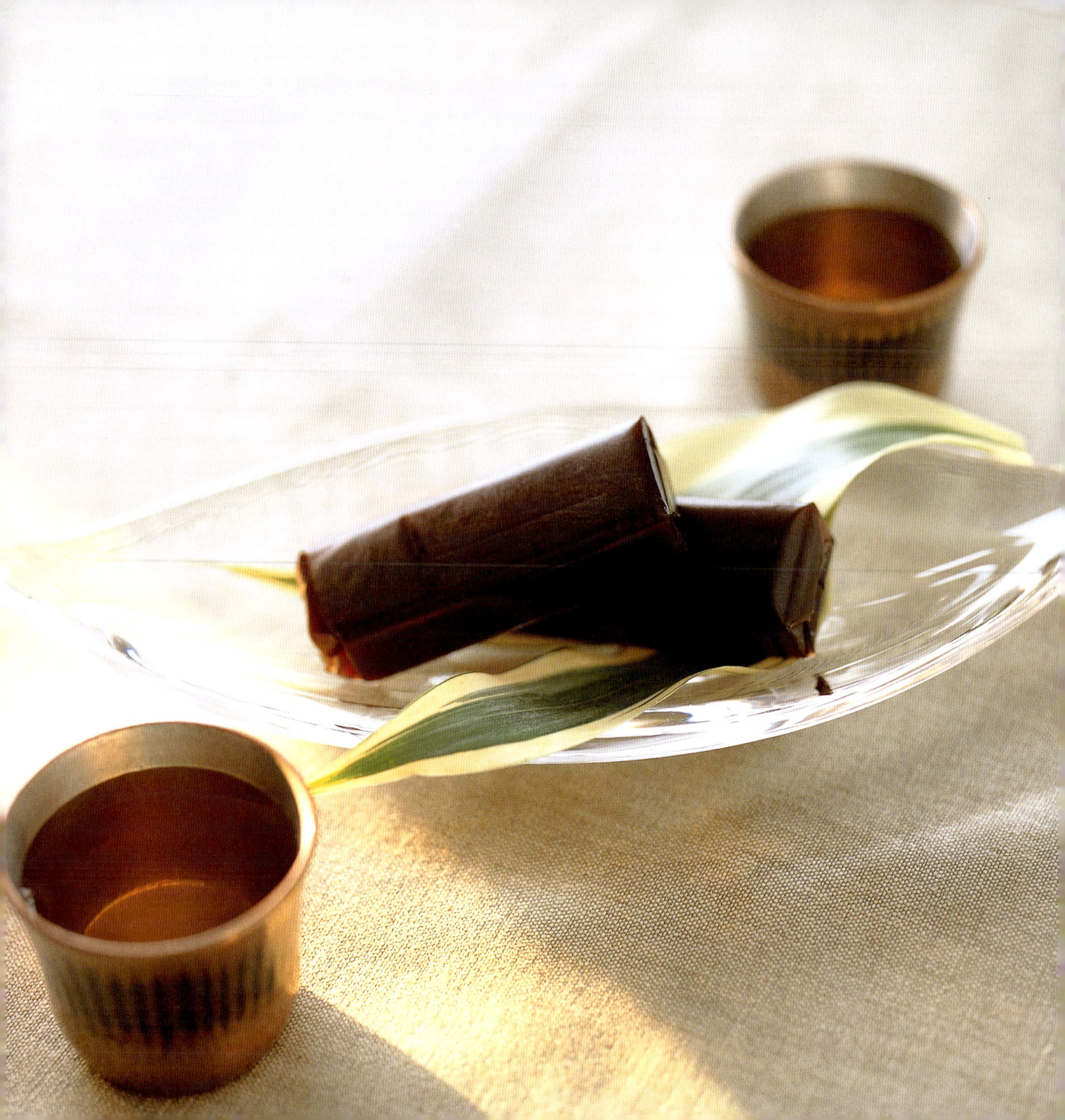

An Afternoon with O-sake 24

日本の伝統菓子と古酒の、古くて新しい楽しみ方
特別純米古酒1988 &
羊羹

「お父さん、お酒でもどう？」。たまには父親と一緒にOsakeを飲んでみたいと思うとき、シンプルなコーディネートながら、こんな中味の濃い取り合わせは、いかがですか。古酒という、日本酒の古くて新しい楽しみ方に、日本の伝統的なスイーツ、羊羹を合わせてみました。懐かしい黒砂糖の香りが、シェリーのような風味を醸し出しているOsakeの香りとよく合い、ゆったりと落ち着いた気分になります。口のなかで溶け合うというよりは、どっしりとした味わいの羊羹が、じっくり少しづつ味わうOsakeの、よき合の手となる組み合わせです。

Tokubetsu Junmai Koshu 1988 & Yokan
"How about drinking o-sake together tonight?" When you feel like drinking with your father, I recommend the simple combination of vintage sake and traditional Japanese desserts, yokan*. The flavor of black sugar marries to the sherry-like aroma of the aged o-sake. If you would like to taste them slowly, it is a good match.

銅製のぐい呑み
銅を打ち出して作る新潟県の伝統工芸品、鎚起（ついき）銅器の器です。味がよりまろやかに。手応えのある重みが、Osakeに風格を添えます。／ぐい呑　縄文　玉川堂Ⓕ／舟形トレイ Sugahara Ⓑ

Copper Guinomi-style Cup
This copper cup is a traditional handcraft of Niigata Prefecture. The tangible weight of the cup makes the taste of o-sake dignified./Guinomi Cup Etched with Jomon (straw-rope) Patterns GYOKUSENDO CO., LTD.Ⓕ／Boat-shaped Tray SUGAHARA GLASSWORKS INC.Ⓑ

羊羹
吟味された材料で作られた羊羹は、スイーツというより、甘味ということばがぴったりな、日本的味わいの原点のひとつ。／小形羊羹「おもかげ」　とらや㉑

Yokan*
Using carefully selected materials, this yokan reminds us of traditional Japan./OMOKAGE TORAYA㉑
*Japanese traditional desserts, made of mainly red beans and sugar.

特別純米古酒1988（福島）
美しい黄金色をしたOsakeは、カレーなどスパイシーな料理の後の食後酒としてもおすすめです。／奥の松酒造（P.95）

Tokubetsu Junmai Koshu 1988 (special junmai aged sake)
This brilliant golden colored o-sake is suitable after eating spicy foods as a digestif./OKUNOMATSU SAKE BREWERY CO., LTD. (P.95)

Essay

スローフードとしてのOsake

　イタリアスローフード協会の会長、カルロ・ペトリーニ氏に、はじめてインタビューをしたのは2000年秋のことです。スローフードということばから、ゆっくり食事をするというイメージや、食の安全性や、食育などのテーマばかりがひとり歩きしているように感じていた当時の私にとって、「スローフードとは自国の食文化を愛することから始まるのです」ということばは、とても印象的でした。つまりそれは、愛するからこそ求める安全性であり、愛するからこそ次世代を育てる食育につながるのだ、と私には理解できたのです。と同時に、"愛することは、表現すること"というイタリア人的な生き方が思い出されました。

　その後、ペトリーニ氏から、「日本人として大切にしている食文化を紹介してほしい」という依頼を受け、2001年に、ペトリーニ氏の故郷であり、スローフード運動発祥の地でもある、イタリア・トリノ近郊の小さな街ブラで、その翌年には、トリノで同協会とピエモンテ州が共催する大規模な食の祭典「サローネ・デル・グスト」で、日本酒を紹介したのです。そのときはじめて本格的な日本酒を飲んだという、イタリア人やその他のヨーロッパ人たちが示した、日本酒への関心の高さには驚かされるものがありました。それはまさに、彼等外国人が、日本酒を通じて日本の食文化を知りたいという思いの表現に他ありませんでした。

　スローフードとしての日本酒が、世界に羽ばたいていくには、まず私たち日本人が、彼等の思いを受けとめ、それを超える情熱をもって、「Osakeを愛すること」がいかに重要なことか、そしてそのことが、「日本の食文化を愛すること」につながるのだということをスローフードは、私に教えてくれたのです。

Osake as a Slow Food

In the year 2000, I interviewed Mr. Carlo Petrini, Chairman of the Italian Slow Food Association for the first time. In those days, when the quality and nutrition of foods were highlighted, he argued that enjoying slow foods derives from loving your own country's food culture. Then I realized that putting importance on chemical-free foods and time-consuming but healhty traditional foods lead to appreciating our own food culture.

He asked me to introduce my cherished Japanese food culture. Therefore, in 2001, to introduce Japanese sake, I visited Bra, a town in the vicinity of *Turin*, Italy, his hometown. Then I participated in *Salone Del Gusto '02*, an international food fair in Turin held by the Slow Food Association and the State of *Piedmont*, in the following year.

Some people there consumed Japanese sake for the first time. They expressed a strong interest in Japanese food culture, as a result of enjoying sake.

This taught me that Japanese should appreciate o-sake much more than they do now in order for o-sake to break into the international arena. In order to be international we should first understand our own culture. The love of o-sake would lead to the appreciation of Japanese food culture overseas.

オーナメント カタツムリ(L)(M)　Sugahara®
Glass Snail(Large/Medium)　SUGAHARA GLASSWORKS INC.®

Scene 5
Digestif with Desserts

もうひとつの時間、
ディジェスティフ

おいしい料理と会話で、お腹も心もたっぷりと満たされた食後のひととき。
食後酒（ディジェスティフ）にOsakeはいかが？
一緒に食卓を囲んだ家族や友人たちと、リビングやテラスに場所を移して、
一杯のお気に入りのOsakeとスイーツを、ゆったりと味わいましょう。
そして、ときにはひとりで、愛読書と共に、深夜の静けさのなかで飲むOsake。
食事の後の、贅沢なもうひとつの時間のはじまりです。

Both heart and stomach are filled with happiness
after delicious cuisine and conversation.
"How about drinking o-sake as a digestif?"
You can enjoy o-sake after dinner with family members or friends,
consuming your favorite o-sake and desserts
in the living room or on the terrace.
Or, how about drinking o-sake at midnight,
while reading your favorite book?
Another pleasurable time will begin.

華 冷酒杯 象彦Ⓝ
Hana Cup for Chilled Sake　ZOHIKO CORPORATIONⓃ

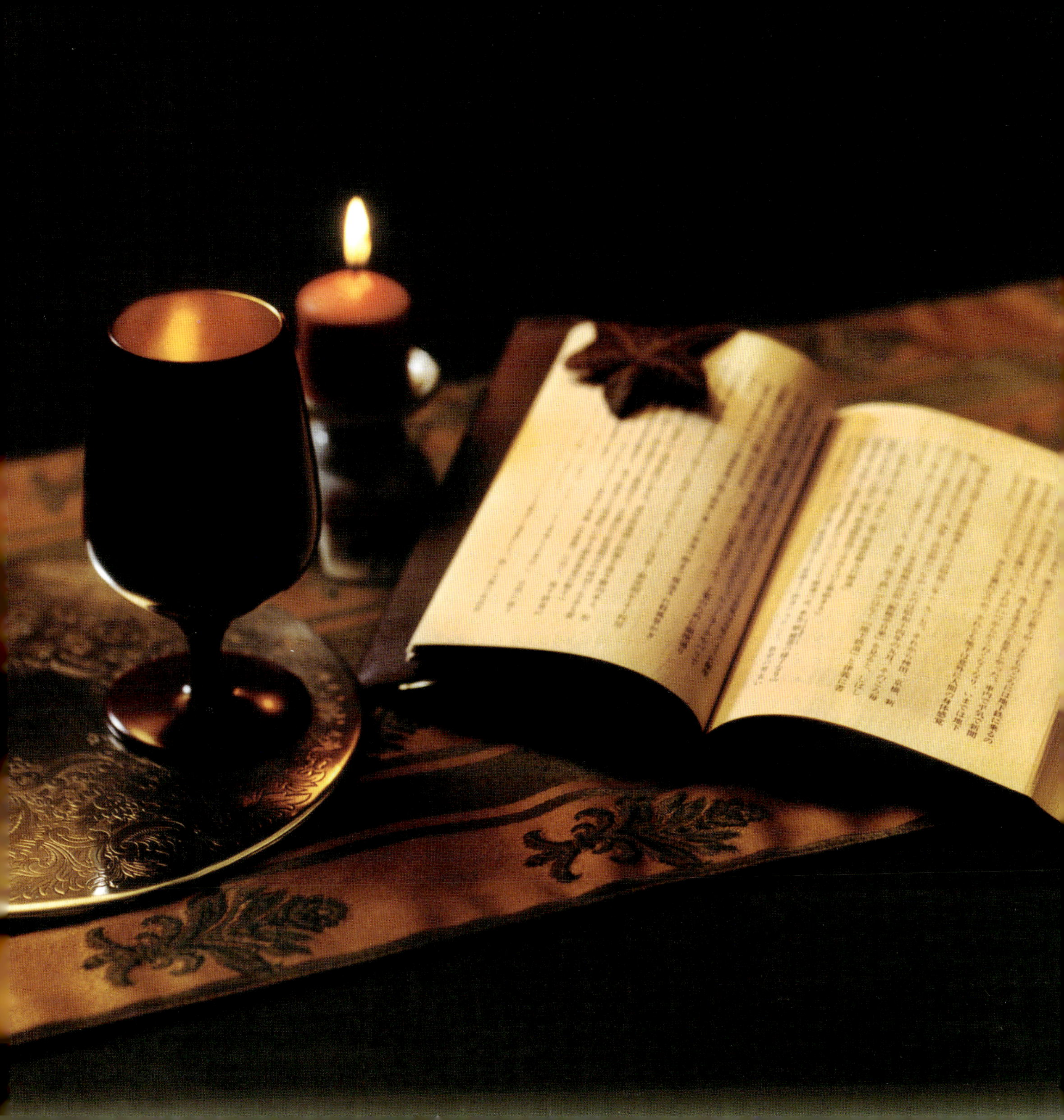

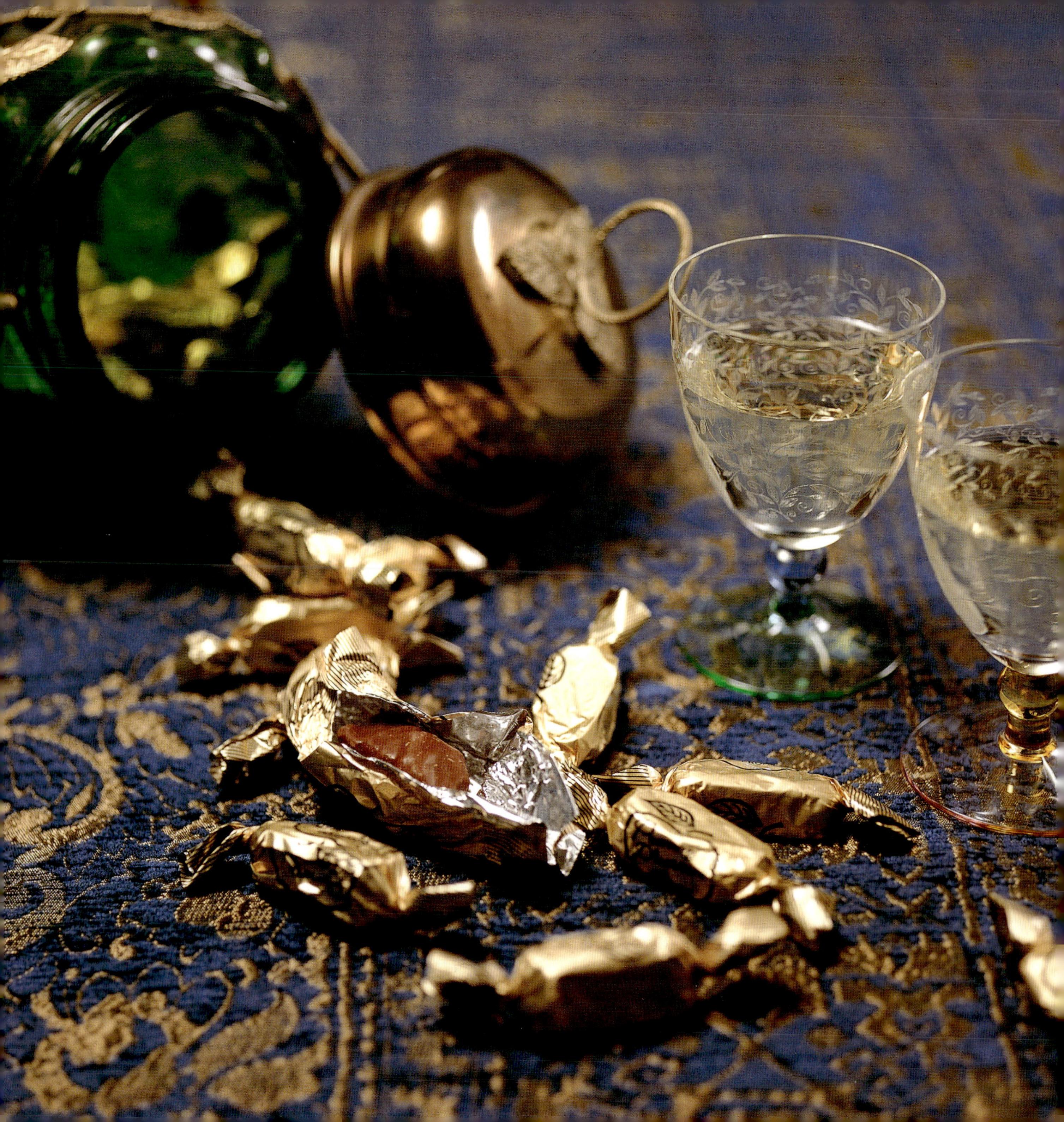

Digestif with Desserts
25

ナイトキャップで、深夜のひととき
貴醸酒＆アップルペースト入りチョコレート

一緒に暮らすパートナーと、眠る前のひととき、ベッドサイドでナイトキャップ。しっかりとしたアルコールを感じさせる甘いOsakeが、チョコレートのほろ苦さを引き出し、大人の時間を演出します。3年の熟成によって生まれたOsakeは、グラスのなかで透明感のある淡いゴールドの輝きを放ちます。京都、東寺の骨董市で見つけたボンボン入れから、チョコレートを取り出すと、オルゴールになっている蓋から、白鳥の湖のメロディーが流れ出します。アコースティックな音色が心地よい、深夜のひとときです。

Kijo-shu & Apple Paste Coated with Chocolate
A night cap with your partner at the bed side. The sweet, strong body of this o-sake goes with the apple paste coated with the slightly bitter taste of chocolate. This combination is most suitable for mature people, I imagine. The light wheat-colored o-sake casts a golden crystal radiance in the glass. When I opened the lid of a bottle of sweets I purchased at an antique fair in Kyoto, the music box inside the bottle began to play a melody from *Swan Lake*. Such an acoustic melody makes us feel entranced.

グラヴィール装飾のグラス
ドイツ、ボヘミア、オーストリア地方で17世紀頃より使われはじめた、ガラス面に彫刻を施すこの技法は、グラスに繊細で複雑な模様を描き出すことを可能にしました。

Gravelines Decoration Glass
The technique of inscribing fine and delicate patterns on glass is said to have been established in the 17th century in Germany, Bohemia, and Austria.

アップルペースト入りチョコレート
蜜でボイルした青リンゴを、ビターチョコで包んだ、甘いものが苦手な人でもつまめる、スイーツです。／ポームダムール　神戸、元町 一番舘㉒

Apple Paste Coated with Chocolate
After boiling a green apple in honey, it is coated with bitter chocolate. Even if you do not have a sweet tooth, you will enjoy this dessert. ／Pomme d'Amour Ichibankan Co., Ltd.㉒

貴醸酒（岩手）
甘く濃厚な味わいながら、後味は、決して甘ったるくなく、ナイトキャップとして、心地よい深い眠りを誘ってくれます。／あさ開（P.92）

Kijo-shu
Sweet, full-bodied and well balanced. The aftertaste is not too sweet. It is good for a nightcap. This o-sake should invite a fast and restful sleep.／Asabiraki Co., Ltd. (P.92)

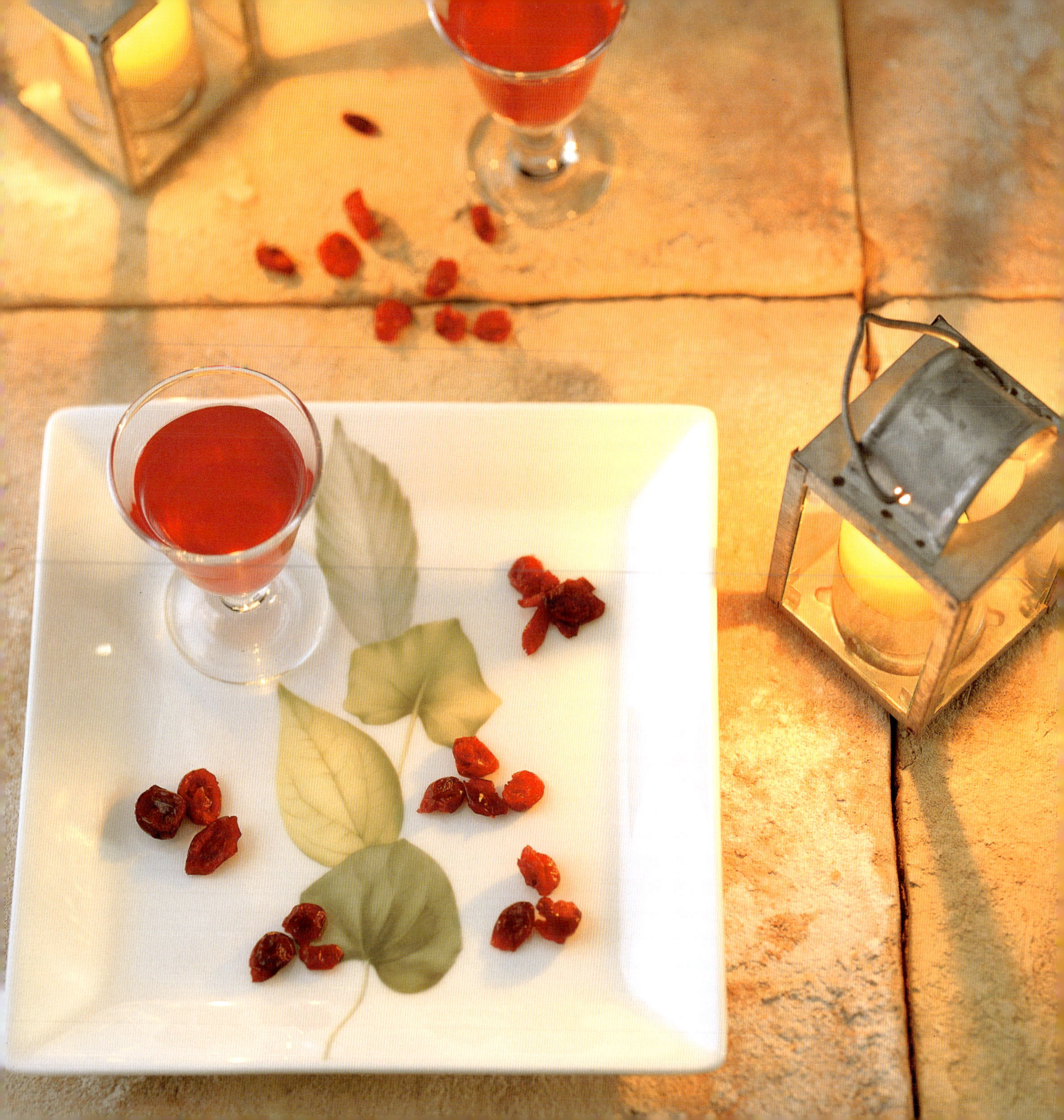

夜風に吹かれてヘルシーカクテル
Osake cocktail サマーヴァカンス&ドライクランベリー

ヴァカンス地の海辺では、気持ちのよい夜風に吹かれながら、ヘルシーなディジェスティフを。活動的な気持ちを象徴するレッドカラーのカクテルとドライクランベリー。ベリーの甘酸っぱさが、さわやかな風味のカクテルのアクセントになって、ついつい食べ過ぎてしまった胃袋を、さっぱりとさせてくれます。素足に感じられる、ひんやりとしたテラコッタの感触が心地よく、お皿の上に、クランベリーで絵を描きながら、長い夏の夜は、まだまだこれからです。

"Summer Vacances" & Dried Cranberries

When you feel a comfortable sea breeze, have a healthy digestif at a resort's beach. Sour cranberries give an accent to the fresh-tasting cocktail. This should enhance digestion after over-eating. I make patterns using cranberries on the plate, and feel the pleasantly cool temperature of the terracotta on my bare feet. The fun of the long night has only started.

四角いお皿
20センチ角ほどのお皿は、中心に描かれたグリーンの葉っぱ模様を生かして、カクテルとおつまみをのせるトレイとして。／20cmスクエアプレート（インザフォレスト）　ニッコー⑤／グラス　日本の酒情報館SAKE PLAZA④

Square Plate
Green leaves are printed on a 20 cm. x 20cm. square plate. When making use of the leaf patterns, use the plate as a tray to serve cocktails and nibbles.／20cm Square Plate(In the Forest)　NIKKO COMPANY⑤／Glass　SAKE PLAZA④

Digestif with Desserts
26

INVIGORATING

ドライクランベリー
アメリカのターキー料理には欠かせない、クランベリーソース。強い酸味も、ドライフルーツとして食べると、カクテルのおつまみにはよく合います。

Dried Cranberries
Cranberry sauce is a must for American turkey cuisine. The strong acidity goes with dry fruits. Excellent with cocktails.

手島麻記子のOsake cocktail サマーヴァカンス
吟醸酒とハチミツ入りのシソジュースを、1:1で混ぜるだけ。消化を助ける働きのあるシソの、すっきりとした味わいが、ディジェスティフにぴったりです。

Makiko Tejima's O-sake Cocktail "Summer Vacances"
Pour ginjo-shu and perilla juice containing honey into a bowl, in the ratio of 1:1 and stir. Perilla facilitates digestion and has a refreshing taste. It is perfect as a digestif.

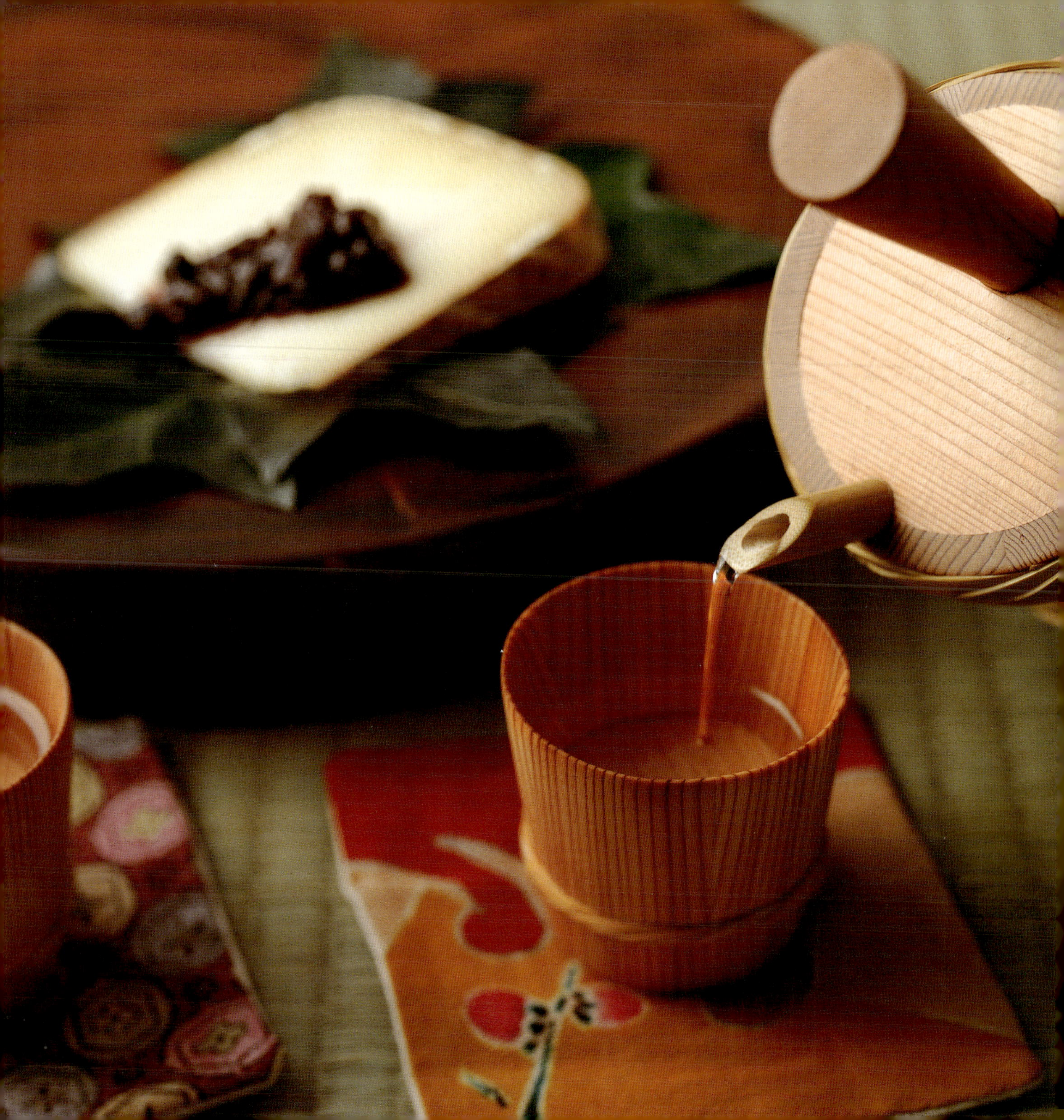

Digestif with Desserts 27

芳醇さとコクが導く、なめらかで深遠な味わい
松竹梅白壁蔵「三谷藤夫」〈山廃純米〉&
オッソー・イラティのブルーベリージャム添え

フランス南西部、スペインとの国境沿いにあるバスク地方では、羊乳のチーズ、オッソー・イラティが特産です。この地方では食後に、このチーズにたっぷりのブルーベリージャムをかけ、力強い地元産の赤ワインと楽しみます。そのあまりのおいしさが忘れられず、芳醇な味わいの山廃純米酒と合わせてみたところ、これがぴったり。Osakeのもつ複雑な酸味と旨味が、チーズのコクと、ブルーベリーの甘酸っぱさに包まれて、なめらかで、より深い味わいとなります。

Mitani Fujio*, Yamahai Junmai-shu & Ossau Iraty with Blueberry Jam

In the southwest part of France, the Basque Provinces are famous for *Ossau Iraty*, a cheese made from ewe's milk. In this district, people enjoy eating the cheese with plenty of blueberry jam, while drinking the strong-bodied local red wine. I tried Yamahai Junmai-shu instead. The complicated acidity and flavor of this o-sake goes well with the rich taste of the cheese and the sweet and sour taste of blueberries.

木の器
樹齢300年近い秋田杉で作られた酒器で飲むOsakeは、味、香り共に、よりまろやかに感じます。栃の木に拭き漆の卓上膳と共に、自然のぬくもりに囲まれて。／酒器 日樽Ⓞ／卓上膳 漆楽Ⓓ

Wooden Tableware
When drinking o-sake with a cup made of 300-year-old cedar, the taste and smell is very mellow. Place a leaf on a lacquerware plate and put a piece of cheese on it. Enjoy eating and drinking, in nature's arms./Sake Cup NittaruⓄ／Dining Tray UrushirakuⒹ

オッソー・イラティ・ブルビ・ピレネー
この変わった名前の由来は、主産地を流れるオッソー川と森林のフォレ・ディラティに由来します。牛乳のタイプもあるので、正式には羊乳という意味の、「ブルビ・ピレネー」が付きます。

Ossau-Iraty-Brebis-Pyrénées
This name derives from the Ossau River and the *Foret d'Iraty* (Forest of Iraty). The French word *brebis* means ewe in English.

松竹梅白壁蔵「三谷藤夫」
〈山廃純米〉（京都）
酒蔵に住む乳酸菌によって、じっくり育てた酒母で仕込んだ山廃仕込み。豊かな風味のある味わいは、40度前後のぬる燗でさらに、ふっくらと。／宝酒造（P.99）

Mitani Fujio* Yamahai Junmai-shu
This o-sake is fermented using rice-malt-yeast mash and lactic bacteria under the *yamahai moto* method. The method eliminates the step of grinding the moto, a highly concentrated yeast mash by first mixing pure koji rice with water to accelerate the process of saccharification and then adding steamed rice. Excellent warmed either to around 40C (104F), or served at room temperature. Full-bodied aftertaste./Takara Shuzo Co., Ltd. (P.99)

---

*The name of this o-sake, Mintani Fujio named after a *touji*, a master brewer.

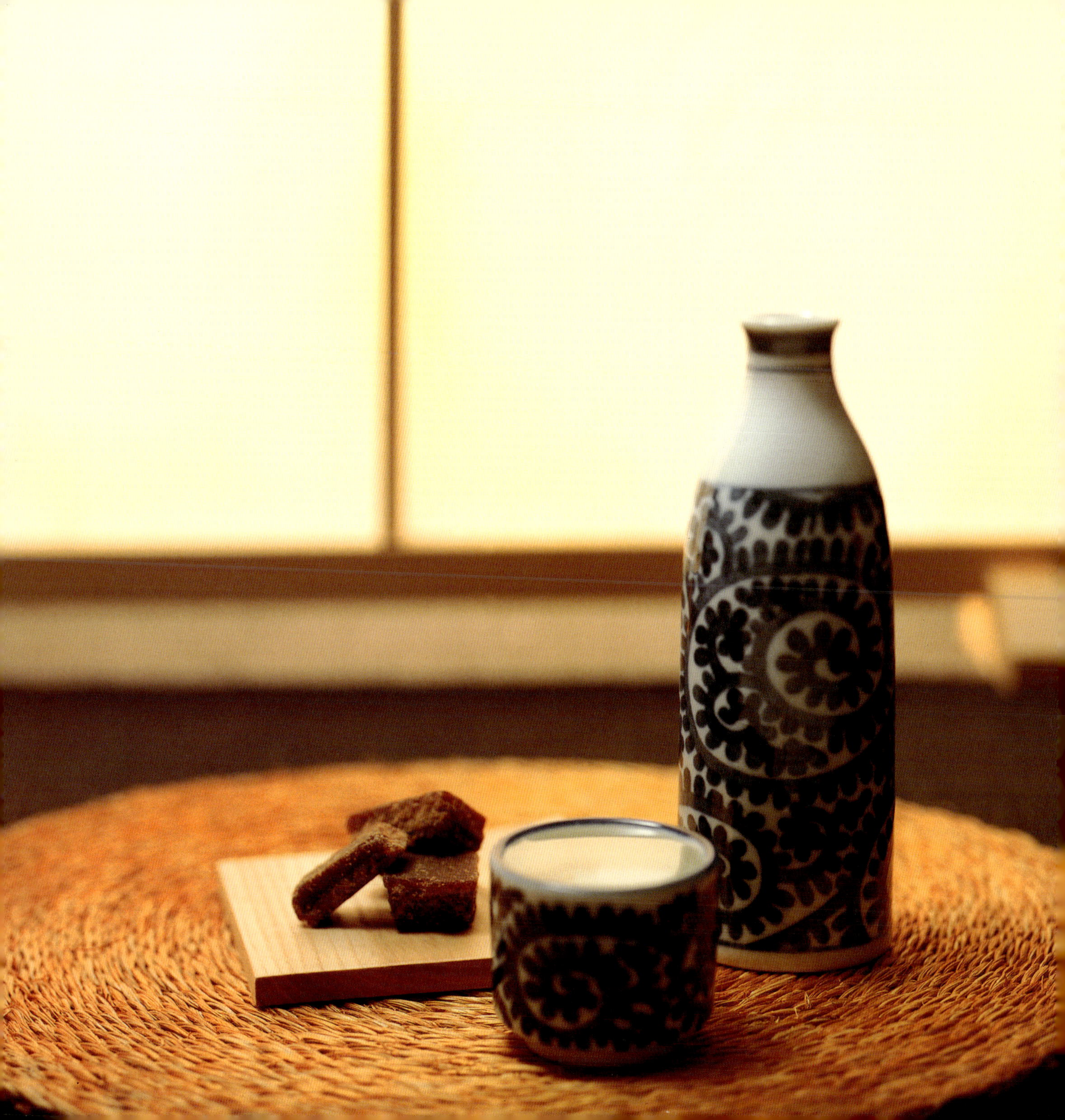

Digestif with Desserts
28

Osakeを囲んで深まる家族の絆
本醸造かほり鶴 昔づくり＆黒糖

ひと昔前、晩酌といえばこんな徳利とお猪口が用意され、イカの塩辛などをつまみにOsakeを飲む父親を囲みながら、家族の夕食が始まったはずです。家族一緒に夕食を食べることさえ間々ならない昨今、眠る前のひととき、パートナーと一緒にOsakeでも飲みながら、子供たちの話を聞く、そんなディジェスティフの時間はいかがですか。醸造アルコールの代わりに、本格焼酎を加えて仕込んだOsake。そのパンチの効いた味わいは、素材そのままともいえる黒砂糖が含む、どっしりとした自然の甘さと、Osakeによって引き出される、隠されたほろ苦さとよく合います。

Honjouzou Kaori Tsuru Mukashi Dukuri & Black Sugar

Nowadays there are not so many occasions for all family members to get together for supper. How about listening to your children talk, while drinking a digestif with your partner? *Shochu*, or distilled spirit is used instead of brewer's alcohol to make this o-sake. Its punchy and slight bitter taste goes with the natural sweet taste of black sugar.

蛸唐草の酒器
渦のように連続した線に点を描いて、まるでタコの足のように見えることから付いた名前。最も親しまれている文様のひとつ。／カネコ小兵製陶所Ⓟ

Octopus Arabesque Patterned Sake Container and Cup
This is named after octopus arms for its curlicue line patterns. It is one of the most popular patterns for dishes and plates.
／KANEKO KO-HYO POTTERY MANUFACTURING CO., LTD.Ⓟ

STIMULANT

黒糖
沖縄で古くから親しまれている、サトウキビの絞り汁をそのまま煮詰めた、カルシウムやカリウムたっぷりの、ヘルシーなスイーツです。

Black Sugar
Sugarcane juice is boiled down to produce black sugar. This is one of the oldest and best sweets in Okinawa.

本醸造かほり鶴 昔づくり（山口）▲
塩を肴に、粋に飲みたいOsakeですが、イタリアのトリッパ（牛胃の煮込み料理）や、日本のトリもつ煮込みともよく合います。ぬる燗もおすすめです。／山縣本店（P.100）

Honjouzou Kaori Tsuru Mukashi Dukuri
It is best with salt, but goes well with *trippa*, or stewed calf stomachs. Good served at a warm or room temperature.
／Yamagata Honten (P.100)

083

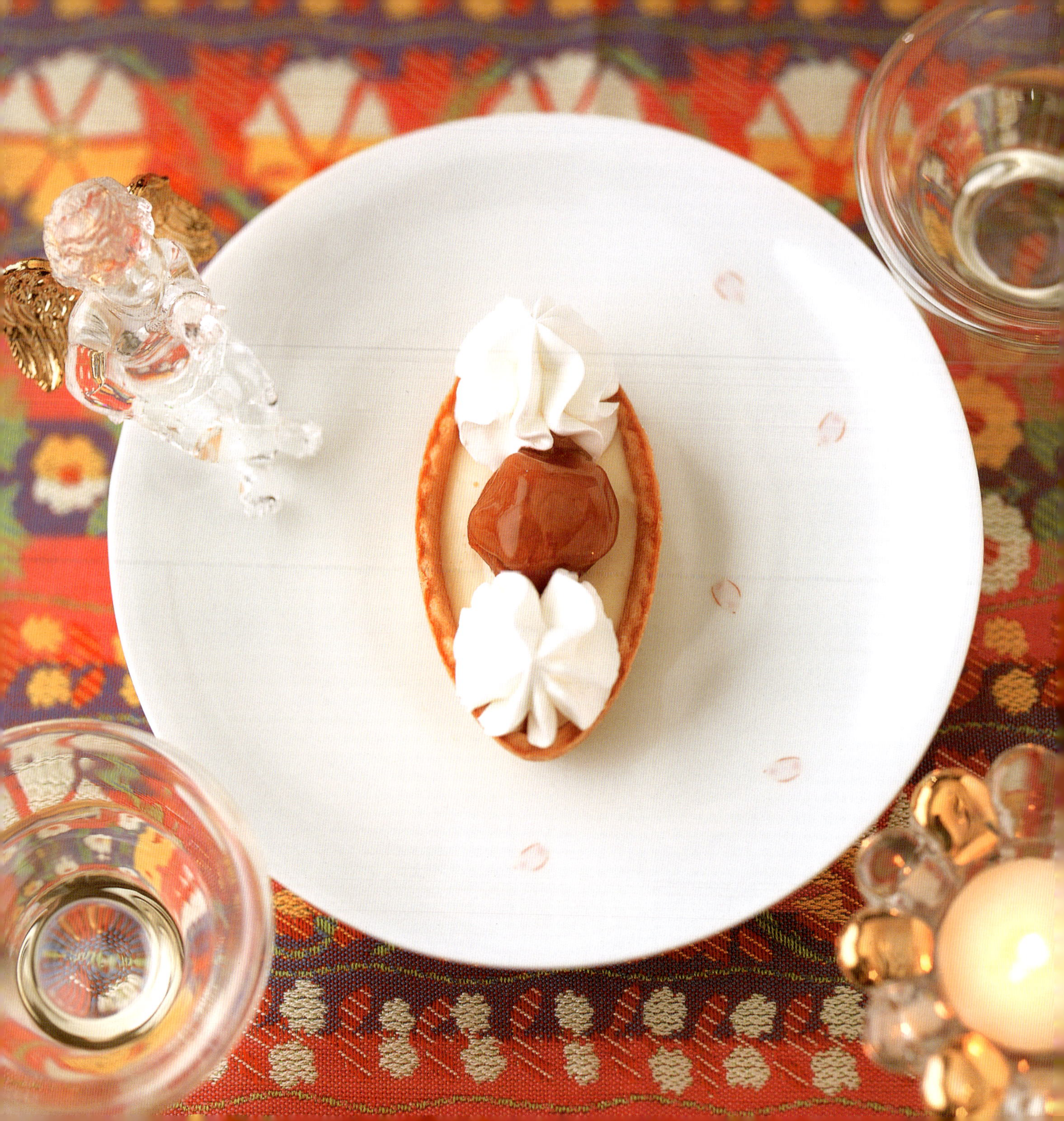

Digestif with Desserts

29

自分へのご褒美。ロマンティックに夢見る夜
福正宗 氷温生貯蔵酒 &
梅干しクリームチーズパイ

よく頑張った自分へのご褒美(ほうび)に、ロマンティックに夢見る甘い夜。生クリームたっぷりのクリームチーズパイに、塩分をかなり抜いた梅干の甘酸っぱい酸味がアクセント。フレッシュな風味の辛口のOsakeと、口のなかでなめらかに溶け合います。お皿にのせたフィギュアの天使が、少女の頃にあこがれたデコレーションケーキを運んできてくれたような、そんな幸せな気分にしてくれます。花びら型のホルダーに灯したキャンドルが、食卓にやさしい陰影を作り出します。

Fukumasamune, Raw Sake Stored Below Freezing & Cream Cheese Pie Garnished with a Pickled Plum

To celebrate your big or small achievements, treat yourselves to a special evening with a cream cheese pie containing a substantial amount of whipped cream. The sweet and sour taste of pickled plums goes pleasantly with the dry taste of this o-sake. The candle in the flower petal shaped holder casts an elegant shadow on the table.

ガラス製のエスプレッソカップ
手に持ったときに熱くないように、二重構造になったフランス製のカップ。キリッと冷やしたOsakeの温度を保つにも、ぴったりです。／AIR CUP　リーン・ロゼ青山®／太鼓鉢 舞桜　玉有©

Espresso Cup Made of Glass
This French cup is designed so as not to convey the hot temperature of coffee to the hand. You can also use it to drink cold o-sake./AIR CUP ligne roset aoyama®/Taiko-bachi Mai-zakura (Drum-shaped bowl) Gyokuyu©

梅干しクリームチーズパイ
食べてみるまでは、この取り合わせがこんなに後を引くおいしさとは信じられない大人気のスイーツです。／シリアルマミー㉓

Cream Cheese Pie Garnished with a Pickled Plum
Before I tried eating this, I did not expect such a nice aftertaste. I was pleasantly surprised. This is a very popular dessert in Japan./cereal mammy㉓

福正宗 氷温生貯蔵酒（石川）▲
揚げ立ての白身魚のフリットや、野菜のてんぷらに、良質な天日塩をつけて食べたくなる、キリッとした飲み口のOsakeです。／福光屋（P.97）

Fukumasamune, Raw Sake Stored Below Freezing
This o-sake has a tangy palate. It should go well with fresh fried white fish fritto and vegetable tempura with sea salt./Fukumitsuya Sake Brewery (P.97)

EUPHORIC

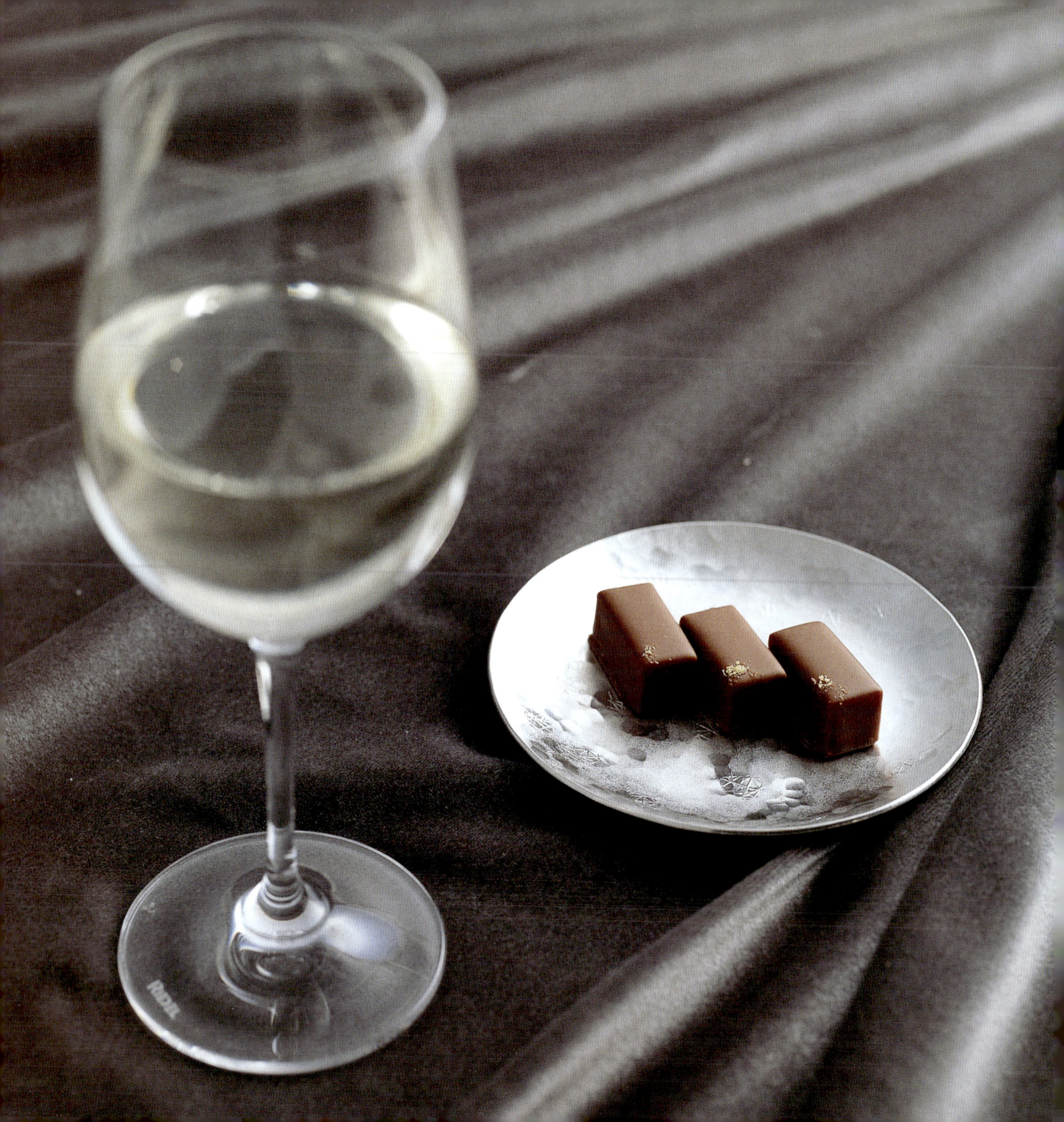

Digestif with Desserts
30

豊かな香りとやわらかな甘味で心地よい眠りに
EXTRA大吟醸 浦霞 &
柚子風味のチョコレート

何となく不完全燃焼だった一日の終わりには、そんな気分をがらりと変えてくれるような、香り高く、切れ味のよいOsakeを飲んで、気持ち良く眠りにつきたいもの。柚子風味の効いたチョコレートの甘さが、Osakeをやわらかに包み込み、柚子の香りと共にすっきりとした味わいに丸みを添えます。低温貯蔵で熟成させたOsakeが放つ馥郁とした香りは、気持ちをゆったりリッチな気分に落ち着かせ、心地よい眠りに導いてくれます。

Extra Dai-ginjo Urakasumi & Citrus Flavored Chocolates

When you feel unfulfilled, why not have a refreshing night cap? This o-sake has a fragrant aroma and a clear taste. The sweet taste of the chocolate with citrus flavor pleasantly overwhelms the flavor of the o-sake. This o-sake has been stored at a low temperature. The bouquet of the o-sake will give you a good night's sleep.

香りを楽しむグラス
日本の蔵元数社と、オーストリアのワイングラスメーカーが開発した大吟醸を味わうためのグラス。唇の触れる、飲み口の繊細なガラスの厚みは、リーデルならでは。／大吟醸グラス リーデル・ジャパン㉒／銘々皿ツチメ 大阪錫器Ⓔ

Glass to Enjoy Aroma
Several Japanese brewers and the Austrian wine glassmaker, RIEDEL, jointly developed this glass to best enjoy drinking dai-ginjo. The ideal thickness of the glass was realized by Riedel's high technology.／Dai-ginjo Glass RIEDEL JAPAN CO., LTD.㉒／Tin Plate Osaka Suzuki Co., Ltd.Ⓔ

柚子風味のチョコレート
柚子の風味が、驚くほど自然にショコラと共に口のなかで溶け合います。並ぶことなしには買えない、大人気ショコラティエの逸品です。／ボンボンショコラ 柚子 ルショコラドゥ アッシュ㉔

Citrus Flavored Chocolates
The flavor of yuzu, a small Japanese citrus fruit, makes a better-than-expected marriage to chocolates. It is hard to buy without waiting in a queue. This is the chocolatier's specialty.／LE CHOCOLAT DE H㉔

EXTRA大吟醸 浦霞（宮城）▲
甘さを含んだ華やかな香りは、クリームソース系のパスタにも似合う、すっきりながら、奥ゆきの深い味わいです。／佐浦（P.93）

Extra Dai-ginjo Urakasumi
The sweetish and mellow flavor of this o-sake marries nicely to cream sauce pasta. This o-sake is superficially simple but mysteriously profound.／Saura Co., Ltd. (P.93)

REGULATING

087

Essay

Osakeとテーブルコーディネート

　ヨーロッパの人たちに、日本人の普段の食卓を紹介するときにいつも感じるのは、私たちの食卓にはいかに「私の…」が多いかということです。お茶碗やお箸はもちろん、湯呑みなど、家族の食卓では銘々の食器が当たり前ですが、欧米ではマグカップ以外に、「My…」というのは、あまり見あたりません。

　ですから、Osakeをすすめるときに、お好きなぐい呑みでどうぞ、と種類が全部違うなかから選んでもらい、食卓を囲む人たちが銘々に違う器でOsakeを楽しむ文化をとても興味深く感じるようです。また、一般的にワインは、グラスで飲みますが、Osakeは、グラス、陶磁器、木（枡）など、さまざまな素材の器で楽しむ文化があります。食卓でいただく自然の恵みを、どんなしつらえで楽しむかを表現するテーブルコーディネートは、その国の食文化のひとつでもあります。酒器とよばれる器には、飲むためのお猪口やぐい呑みをはじめ、注ぐための徳利やお銚子、片口など、豊富な種類やデザインがあります。どんな酒器で飲むかによって、味そのものが変化するのはもちろんですが、「目で味わう楽しさ」が、食卓を囲む人たちの気持ちをとても豊かにしてくれます。

　何かと忙しい今の時代だからこそ、そんな日々の暮らしのなかの豊かさを大切にしていきたいと思うのです。

O-sake and Table Settings

Every time I introduce Japanese casual table settings to Europeans, I notice that Japanese people like to use his or her own specific cup, chopsticks, and so on. In Europe, other than mugs, they don't usually have specific plates or cutlery.

It may be interesting to serve o-sake in different cups and ask your guests to choose their favorite ones. Generally speaking, unlike wines, o-sake can be served in glasses, porcelain cups, traditional wooden cups (masu), and so on. How you enjoy the blessings of nature at the dining table reflects your country's culture and your own tastes.

There is a variety of goods for o-sake both in type and design: small sake-cups, guinomi-style cup, tokkuri, sake decanter, lipped sake ware, and so on. A cup or a container changes the flavor of o-sake and enriches people at the dining table, giving delight to their eyes. In the midst of a hectic life, I want to cherish such pleasure in my daily life.

青交趾さくらぐい呑み　青交趾チロリ　洸春陶苑Ⓛ
Blue Kouchi Cherry Blossoms Guinomi-style Cup　Kousyun TouenⓁ

O-sake Makers' Profiles

スイーツに似合うOsake銘鑑

バラエティに富んだOsakeの味に出合うと、Osake自体のことはもちろん、蔵元や杜氏についてなど、その味が生まれるに至ったさまざまなことを知りたくなります。そしてやがては、日本の風土によって育まれたOsakeの故郷を訪ねる、そんな旅に出かけたくなるかもしれません。このOsake銘鑑は、スイーツに似合うOsakeの味わいを、さらに深めるための手引きとして、また、本書で紹介したOsakeとまったく同じものが手に入らなかったときに、そのOsakeと似たタイプのものを探す際に、活用してください。

List of Sake that Goes Well with Desserts
Every time I encounter o-sake with diverse tastes,
I come to want to know more about the o-sake itself,
and its brewer, touji*, production processes, etc.
Over time, I may visit the region which nurtured the o-sake.
To deepen the profundity of the taste of
each o-sake that admirably marries desserts,
and to find alternative o-sake that you can not find the
same o-sake introduced in this book,
please use the following information as a guide.

*Touji (Toji) are the master brewers of the traditional sake kura (Edo period breweries),
the elite of a unique breed of artisans who trace their roots to the Edo period.

蔵元MAP

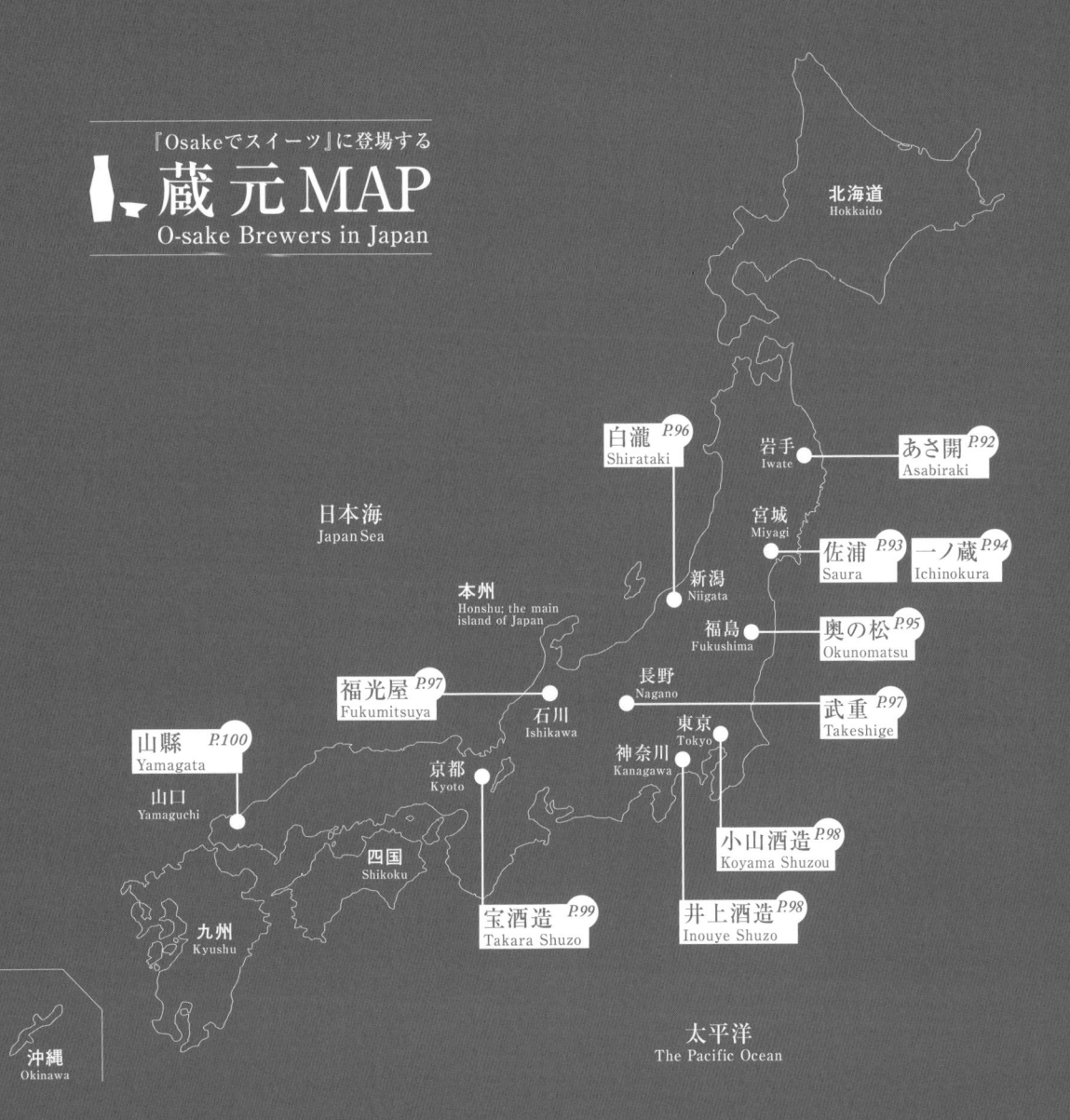

『Osakeでスイーツ』に登場する
O-sake Brewers in Japan

北海道 Hokkaido

白瀧 P.96 Shirataki
岩手 Iwate
あさ開 P.92 Asabiraki

日本海 Japan Sea

宮城 Miyagi
佐浦 P.93 Saura
一ノ蔵 P.94 Ichinokura

新潟 Niigata

本州 Honshu; the main island of Japan

福島 Fukushima
奥の松 P.95 Okunomatsu

福光屋 P.97 Fukumitsuya
石川 Ishikawa
長野 Nagano
武重 P.97 Takeshige

東京 Tokyo
神奈川 Kanagawa

山縣 P.100 Yamagata
山口 Yamaguchi

京都 Kyoto

四国 Shikoku

小山酒造 P.98 Koyama Shuzou

宝酒造 P.99 Takara Shuzo
井上酒造 P.98 Inouye Shuzo

九州 Kyushu

沖縄 Okinawa

太平洋 The Pacific Ocean

091

あさ開（岩手）

「南部杜氏」の名と共に広く知られる酒どころ岩手の伝統ある蔵元。明治4年の創業以来、匠の技をしっかりと受け継ぎながら、常に時代の求める酒造りに取り組んでいる。蔵のある敷地は観光酒蔵として一般に開放。白壁の土蔵と瓦屋根の仕込蔵見学をはじめ、レストランやカフェなどもあり、さまざまな角度から酒の楽しみ方を提案している。太い柱と梁が張り巡らされた明治時代の蔵を再生した源三屋ではコンサートも開かれる。

Asabiraki (Iwate Prefecture)
Established in 1871, more than a hundred years ago, developing esoteric techniques since then. Renowned for the name, Nanbu-touji. Responsive to the changes in taste of the times. Its storerooms are open to the public. There is a restaurant and a café. Concerts are held in one of the store rooms.

岩手 Iwate

株式会社あさ開
岩手県盛岡市大慈寺町10番34号
Tel. 019-652-3111(代)
www.asabiraki-net.jp
Asabiraki Co., Ltd.
10-34, Daijiji-cho,
Morioka City,
Iwate Prefecture

RIZa（純米酒）

RIZは、フランス語でお米のこと。RIZaは発酵中に生まれる炭酸ガスをそのまま閉じ込めた、低アルコールのスパークリングタイプの日本酒。しっとりと、キメの細かな泡にも純米のほわっとした丸みのある味わいがある。

- アルコール度数：6度以上7度未満　原材料：米・米こうじ　精米歩合：65%　酸度*2：2.0　日本酒度*1：−20
- 希望小売価格：504円（320ml）　味のタイプ：甘口

RIZa
Named after the French word *riz*, rice. Low alcohol, sparkling Japanese sake. Fine bubbles create a subtle mellow flavor.

- Alcohol: From 6% to less than 7%
- Ingredients: Rice and malted rice
- Rice milling percentage: 65%
- Acid degree*2: 2.0
- Sake meter value*1: −20
- Recommended retail price: 504 yen (320 ml)
- Type of taste: Sweet

大吟醸ライト 水の王（大吟醸酒）

その名の通り盛岡三清水の清らかさそのままに、水よりもみずみずしい大吟醸酒。超低温発酵により"さらりと流れて、ふわりと薫る"新しい味わいが特徴。クリアで未来的な造形のボトルとシルバーのパッケージがおしゃれでスタイリッシュ。

- アルコール度数：10度以上11度未満　原材料：米・米こうじ・醸造アルコール　精米歩合：50%　酸度：1.2　日本酒度：−3　希望小売価格：1,260円（400ml）　味のタイプ：やや甘口

Miz no Eau
Choice brew. Made from thoroughly polished rice and uses some of the purest water in Morioka City, Iwate Prefecture. Fermented under extremely low temperatures. Accordingly, the flavor hangs in the air like a cloud. Clear taste and goes down smoothly. Silver package and transparent bottle look futuristic.

- Alcohol: From 10% to less than 11%
- Ingredients: Rice, malted rice, and brewer's alcohol
- Rice milling percentage: 50%
- Acid degree: 1.2
- Sake meter value: −3
- Recommended retail price: 1,260 yen (400 ml)
- Type of taste: Slightly sweet

貴醸酒

仕込みの際に、米・米こうじに「水」ではなく、「純米原酒」を使用して醸造したもの。3年間の熟成により育まれた芳香が特徴。淡い金色に熟成した、甘く濃い味わいの日本酒。

- アルコール度数：16度以上17度未満　原材料：米・米こうじ　精米歩合：65%　酸度：3.1　日本酒度：−45
- 希望小売価格：866円（300ml）　味のタイプ：甘口

Kijoushu
Pure rice liquor is used instead of water. Fabulous aroma developed through three years of maturation. Light gold color. Sweet and full-bodied.

- Alcohol: From 16% to less than 17%
- Ingredients: Rice and malted rice.
- Rice milling percentage: 65%
- Acid degree: 3.1
- Sake meter value: −45
- Recommended retail price: 866 yen (300 ml)
- Type of taste: Sweet

---

*1 「日本酒度」は、水（±0）に対する酒の比重を「日本酒度計」で計ったものです。この比重は、糖分を中心とするエキス分が多い酒になるほど重くなりマイナス（ー）に、エキス分が少ない酒になるほど軽くなり、プラス（＋）に傾きます。

*1 The palate of Japanese sake consists of complicated tastes, such as sweetness, acidity, dryness, bitterness, and astringency. The simplest guide to dryness and sweetness is called Nihonshu-do, or the sake meter value. The value is a measure of the amount of residual sugar and alcohol in sake. The sake meter works on the principle that alcohol is lighter than water while glucose is heavier. A positive sake meter value indicates less residual sugar and thus drier sake. A negative value indicates that the sake will be sweeter.

佐浦（宮城）

1724年（享保9年）の創業。「丁寧に造って丁寧に売る」を基本に、高品質の酒造りを目指している。機械やステンレスざるの洗米が多い現在でも、吟醸酒には「竹ざる」を使った洗米・浸漬（しんせき）・水切りを採用し、進化した酒造りの技術のなかに、生身の人間の感触や勘にこだわりをもつ。「浦霞」の銘柄名は、塩釜を詠んだ源実朝の歌「塩釜の浦の松風霞むなり八十島かけて春や立つらむ」に由来し、大正時代に名付けられた。東北最古のゴルフコースも有する蔵元。

Saura（Miyagi Prefecture）
Established in 1724. Aims at producing o-sake of high quality. Produces o-sake putting importance on the five senses and using traditional tools. The brand name Urakasumi comes from a line in a tanka (an old Japanese poem) from the 13th century describing a rural place in Miyagi. By the way, Saura is known for having the oldest golf course in Tohoku, in northern Japan.

株式会社佐浦
宮城県塩釜市本町2-19
Tel. 022-362-4165
www.urakasumi.com
Saura Co., Ltd
2-19, Moto-machi,
Shiogama City,
Miyagi Prefecture.

浦霞禅（純米吟醸酒）
浦霞禅という酒銘と、ラベルと化粧箱の禅画は、結果的には実現されなかったが、昭和40年代後半に、その頃禅に対する関心が高まっていたフランスへの輸出を考えて考案されたもの。程よい香りとまろやかな味わいのバランスのとれた飲みやすい純米吟醸酒。

- アルコール度数：15度以上16度未満
- 原材料：米・米こうじ
- 精米歩合：50%
- 酸度：1.3
- 日本酒度：+1.0
- 希望小売価格：2,247円（720ml）
- 味のタイプ：辛口

Urakasumi Zen
Named after the Zen boom in France in the 1970s. Moderate bouquet and mild palate. Well-balanced and highly drinkable Junmai-ginjo-shu.

- Alcohol: From 15% to less than 16%
- Ingredients: Rice and malted rice
- Rice milling percentage: 50%
- Acid degree: 1.3
- Sake meter value: +1.0
- Recommended retail price: 2,247 yen (720 ml)
- Type of taste: Dry

萩の白露（純米酒）
宮城県で開発された低アルコールタイプ純米酒酵母「宮城酵母・愛実（まなみ）」と宮城の酒造好適米「蔵の華」で醸し出した、甘酸っぱくてさわやかな純米酒。女性向けのお酒に特有の水っぽさを感じさせない、旨味のあるおいしさたっぷりのお酒。ライトブルーのボトルが清涼感を感じさせる。

- アルコール度数：9度以上10度未満
- 原材料：米・米こうじ
- 精米歩合：60%
- 酸度：2.7
- 日本酒度：-40
- 希望小売価格：588円（300ml）
- 味のタイプ：甘口

Hagi no Shiratsuyu
(Dew of Japanese bush clover)
Made using locally developed low alcohol junmai-shu yeast and local rice, Kuranohana. The light blue color of the bottle looks cool.

- Alcohol: From 9% to less than 10%
- Ingredients: Rice and malted rice
- Rice milling percentage: 60%
- Acid degree: 2.7
- Sake meter value: −40
- Recommended retail price: 588 yen (300 ml)
- Type of taste: Sweet

EXTRA大吟醸 浦霞（大吟醸酒）
さらりとした喉越し、透明感のある吟醸香で、湧き水のように上質でキレイな日本酒。日本酒には珍しいコルク栓。ワイン感覚のボトルとラベル。開栓時は付属のコルクスクリューで開ける。毎年限定出荷なので、日本酒好きの方へプレゼントしても喜ばれそう。

- アルコール度数：16度以上17度未満
- 原材料：米・米こうじ・醸造アルコール
- 精米歩合：40%
- 酸度：1.1～1.3
- 日本酒度：+4.0～+5.0
- 希望小売価格：3,980円（720ml）
- 味のタイプ：やや辛口

Extra Dai-ginjo Urakasumi
Goes down smoothly. Transparent like spring water. Clear bouquet. The bottle and label look like those used for wine. Only available in limited production. Excellent as a gift for Japanese sake lovers.

- Alcohol: From 16% to less than 17%
- Ingredients: Rice, malted rice, and brewer's alcohol
- Rice milling percentage: 40%
- Acid degree: Between 1.1 and 1.3
- Sake meter value: Between +4.0 and +5.0
- Recommended retail price: 3,980 yen (720 ml)
- Type of taste: Slightly dry

---

*2「酸度」は、酒中の有機酸（乳酸、コハク酸、リンゴ酸など）の量を表わしています。有機酸は、酒の味に酸味、旨味をもたらします。また、日本酒度のマイナスの数字が大きいほど濃醇で甘く、プラスの数字が大きいほど淡麗で辛い傾向にあるといわれますが、実際には、酸度にも影響されます。日本酒度が同じ酒で比べると、酸度が高いほど甘味が打ち消されて辛く、逆に酸度が低いと甘く感じます。

*2 Acid degree indicates the concentration of organic acid such as lactic acid, succinic acid, and malic acid in sake. An organic acid brings acidity and flavor to sake. You will get a better idea of how sake will taste if you can also obtain information about its acidity, as this greatly affects dryness and sweetness.

一ノ蔵（宮城）

昭和48年に4つの蔵元がひとつになり、誕生したのが一ノ蔵。以来、自然との共生、伝統、地域振興を原点に、年間で一升瓶にして200万本分の酒を仕込みながらも、手造りの酒造りに取り組んでいる。一方、低アルコール酒の火付け役ともなった「すず音」の開発や、ライスパワーエキスを用いた商品開発、食の安全・安心を理念にした「良い食品づくりの会」への加盟など、時代に則した新たな挑戦の数々にはいつも勢いが感じられる。

Ichinokura（Miyagi Prefecture）
Four sake brewers merged into one in 1973. Keen on ecology, tradition, nutrition, safety, and regional industry development. Produces 2 million bottles (1.8l) of o sake annually and develops low-alcohol sake like Suzune. Innovates in accordance with the changes of the times.

宮城 Miyagi

株式会社一ノ蔵
宮城県志田郡
松山町千石字大欅14
Tel.0229-55-3322
www.ichinokura.co.jp
Ichinokura Co., Ltd.
14, Ohkeyaki, Sengoku,
Matsuyama-machi,
Shida-gun, Miyagi Prefecture

一の蔵 米米酒

日本酒ライスパワー・ネットワークによって開発された「ライスパワーエキスNo.101」は、胃潰瘍の予防、治療に効果があることが確認されています。従来の日本酒のイメージからは離れた、フルーティーな味わいは、健康志向が強まる現代におすすめです。

- ■アルコール度数:6.5～7.5度
- ■原材料:米・米こうじ・No.101米エキス
- ■精米歩合:65%
- ■酸度:3.5～4.5
- ■日本酒度:－65～－75
- ■希望小売価格:1,155円(500ml)
- ■味のタイプ:甘口

Komekome Shu
Produces sake using anti-ulcer rice nutrients "Rice power essence No.101". Unprecedentedly fruity taste. Good for health-conscious drinkers.

- ■Alcohol: Between 6.5% and 7.5%
- ■Ingredients: Rice, malted rice, and power nutrients
- ■Rice milling percentage: 65%
- ■Acid degree: Between 3.5 and 4.5
- ■Sake meter value: Between −65 and −75
- ■Recommended retail price: 1,155 yen (500 ml)
- ■Type of taste: Sweet

すず音

淡雪にも似た薄にごりの「すず音」は、グラスに注ぐと繊細で涼しげな泡が立ちのぼる発泡性の日本酒。低アルコール酒の残糖分を瓶内で再発酵させ炭酸ガスを封じ込めた一ノ蔵オリジナル製法。凛とした気品のある、優しい味わい。

- ■アルコール度数:4.5～5.5度
- ■原材料:米・米こうじ
- ■精米歩合:65%
- ■酸度:3.0～4.0
- ■日本酒度:－70～－90
- ■希望小売価格:735円(300ml)
- ■味のタイプ:甘口

Suzune
Fuzzy white color like light snow. Sparkling sake. Produced with its proprietary method.
Delicate and graceful taste.

- ■Alcohol: Between 4.5% and 5.5%
- ■Ingredients: Rice and malted rice
- ■Rice milling percentage: 65%
- ■Acid degree: Between 3.0 and 4.0
- ■Sake meter value: Between −70 and −90
- ■Recommended retail price: 735 yen (300 ml)
- ■Type of taste: Sweet

奥の松（福島）

享保元年1716年創業。安達太良山の伏流水豊かな、酒どころ二本松に蔵を構え、飲みやすく味のある酒として、各地の鑑評会で毎年のように優等賞を受賞する、伝統と技の蔵元。「オンザテーブル」の日本酒をイメージしてデザインされたオリジナルボトルは、持ちやすくシンプル。蔵を代表する最高ランクの酒のラベルには郷土の伝統工芸品である手漉き和紙を使用するなど、酒のおいしさを前提にした、デザインへのこだわりが感じられる。

Oku no Matsu（Fukushima Prefecture）
Established in 1716. Located in Nihonmatsu, near Mt. Adatara. Very drinkable. Earns honor prizes almost every year. The designs of its o-sake bottles are simple, using handmade Japanese paper, and local traditional handcrafts.

福島 Fukushima

奥の松酒造株式会社
福島県二本松市長命69番地
Tel.0243-22-2153
www.okunomatsu.co.jp
OKUNOMATSU SAKE BREWERY CO., LTD.
69, Choumei, Nihon-matsu City, Fukushima Prefecture.

純米大吟醸 FN（純米大吟醸酒）

カーレース、フォーミュラ・ニッポンの表彰式で勝利の美酒として選ばれた唯一の日本酒。デラウエア種のブドウのような淡く若々しい果実香と舌先に踊る軽快なガスが、程よい緊張感とエレガンスを感じさせる瓶内発酵の純米大吟醸酒。

■アルコール度数：11度以上12度未満　■原材料：米・米こうじ　■精米歩合：40%　■酸度：2.5　■日本酒度：-25　■希望小売価格：5,250円（720ml）、10,500円（1600ml）　■味のタイプ：甘口

Junmai Dai-ginjo FN
The only o-sake chosen for winners of Formula Nippon races in Japan. Sparkling sake. Gentle, youthful flavor creates elegance.

■Alcohol: From 11% to less than 12%
■Ingredients: Rice and malted rice
■Rice milling percentage: 40%
■Acid degree: 2.5
■Sake meter value: -25
■Recommended retail price:
   5,250 yen (720 ml)
   10,500 yen (1600 ml)
■Type of taste: Sweet

木桶仕込純米酒（純米酒）

昔は当たり前だった木桶仕込み。酒造りの効率化によって昭和30年代に途絶えてしまった仕込み方法を現代の技術で復活させ造られた伝統的で新しい日本酒。発酵を木製の桶で行うため、複雑な味わいをもったお酒に仕上がっている。6月以降発売。

■アルコール度数：15度以上16度未満　■原材料：米・米こうじ　■精米歩合：60%　■酸度：1.8　■日本酒度：-4.5　■希望小売価格：3,150円（720ml）　■味のタイプ：やや甘口

Kioke Jikomi Junmai-shu
Made using wooden casks according to the traditional method. This method vanished in the 1950s when the industry promoted modernizing production methods. The brewer returned to the traditional method. Complicated palate.

■Alcohol: From 15%
   to less than 16%
■Ingredients: Rice and malted rice
■Rice milling percentage: 60%
■Acid degree: 1.8
■Sake meter value: -4.5
■Recommended retail price:
   3,150 yen (720 ml)
■Type of taste: Slightly sweet

特別純米古酒 1988

やや甘口の特別純米酒を熟成させた古酒。時の流れを感じさせる、紹興酒のような濃熟な風味と純米酒ならではの丸みのある味わいが絶妙。透明なボトルに輝く琥珀色の酒がとても美しい。食中はもちろんのこと、ゆったりとした時間のなかで食後に楽しむ酒として最適。

■アルコール度数：15度以上16度未満　■原材料：米・米こうじ　■精米歩合：60%　■酸度：2.0　■日本酒度：-6　■希望小売価格：5,250円（720ml）　■味のタイプ：甘口

Tokubetsu Junmai Koshu（1988）
Sweetish aged sake.
Rich and full-bodied, round taste. The amber color of this o-sake looks exquisite in the transparent bottle. Good for serving during a meal or as a digestif.

■Alcohol: From 15% to less
   than 16%
■Ingredients: Rice and malted rice
■Rice milling percentage: 60%
■Acid degree: 2.0
■Sake meter value: -6
■Recommended retail price:
   5,250 yen (720 ml)
■Type of taste: Sweet

白瀧（新潟）

江戸時代末期に創業。吟醸酒ブームをまきおこした白瀧酒造きっての銘柄「上善如水」のほかにも、現在の白瀧酒造の初代創業者の名が付いた「湊屋藤助」も新潟県内限定発売の酒として人気。クッキングスクールやシーズン毎のイベントなど、全国展開の若い世代へのPR活動も積極的。自社のホームページには日本酒を使ったカクテルレシピが20種以上も紹介されており、従来の日本酒の飲み方にとらわれない新しい楽しみ方の提案もしている。

Shirataki（Niigata Prefecture）
Established in late Edo period, in the 19th century. One of its specialties, Jozen Mizu no Gotoshi created a ginjo-shu boom. Minatoya Tousuke, named after the brewery founder is also popular. Develops proactive PR activities throughout Japan. Keen in developing new o-sake cocktails.

新潟 Niigata

白瀧酒造株式会社
新潟県南魚沼郡湯沢町大字湯沢2640番地
Tel.0120-858520
http://www.jozen.co.jp
SHIRATAKI SAKE BREWERY CO., LTD.
2640,Yuzawa,Yuzawa-town
Minami-uonuma-gun,
Niigata Prefecture.

大吟醸 霊泉汲不盡（大吟醸酒）

はじまりは良い水と良く磨いた米が溶け合うことで放つ甘く、クリーミーな香り。それに、ふくよかな甘味、まろやかな酸味によるふくらみのある味わいが続く大吟醸酒。

■アルコール度数：16度以上17度未満　■原材料：米・米こうじ・醸造アルコール　■精米歩合：40％　■酸度：1.2　■日本酒度：＋4　■希望小売価格：5,250円（720ml）、10,500円（1800ml）　■味のタイプ：やや辛口

Dai-ginjo（Grand-ginjo）
Reisen Kumedomo Tsukizu
Sweet and creamy bouquet comes first and then round sweetness and acidity follows.
■Alcohol: From 16% to less than 17%
■Ingredients: Rice, malted rice, and brewer's alcohol
■Rice milling percentage: 40%
■Acid degree: 1.2
■Sake meter value: +4
■Recommended retail price:
 5,250 yen（720 ml）,
 10,500 yen（1800 ml）
■Type of taste: Slightly dry

吟醸 上善如水（吟醸酒）

スタイリッシュで透明感のあるボトルデザインと共に、一躍有名になった吟醸酒。口当たりと香りは、たおやかでありながらフレッシュ。軽やかな甘味と控え目な酸味が瑞々しさを印象づける。水の良さからくる上品な味わいのお酒。

■アルコール度数：14度以上15度未満　■原材料：米・米こうじ・醸造アルコール　■精米歩合：60％　■酸度：1.3　■日本酒度：＋5　■希望小売価格：262円（150ml）、612円（300ml）、1,325円（720ml）、2,650円（1800ml）　■味のタイプ：やや辛口

Ginjo Jozen Mizu no Gotoshi
Jumped to stardom with a stylish and clear bottle design. Fresh and mild palate and nose. Slight sweetness and acidity are distinctively bracing.
■Alcohol: From 14% to less than 15%
■Ingredient: Rice, malted rice, and brewer's alcohol
■Rice milling percentage: 60%
■Acid degree: 1.3
■Sake meter value: +5
■Recommended retail price:
 262 yen（150 ml）,
 612 yen（300 ml）,
 1,325 yen（720 ml）,
 2,650 yen（1800 ml）
■Type of taste: Slightly dry

純米 上善如水（純米酒）

上善如水の純米酒。ビタミンカラー、オレンジ色のモダンなパッケージとラベルが上善のイメージを変えた。軟らかで上質な水で仕込んだ、さわやかで透明感のあるお酒。純米ならではのピュアな味わい、ほのかな甘さが特徴。

■アルコール度数：13度以上14度未満　■原材料：米・米こうじ　■精米歩合：60％　■酸度：1.4　■日本酒度：－1　■希望小売価格：189円（150ml）、420円（300ml）、997円（720ml）、2,100円（1800ml）　■味のタイプ：やや甘口

Junmai Jozen Mizu no Gotoshi
Pure rice sake. The vivid orange color of the modern package and label changed the traditional image of conventional Jozen Mizu no Gotoshi. Made using soft water. Fresh and clear. Slightly sweet.
■Alcohol: From 13% to less than 14%
■Ingredients: Rice and malted rice
■Rice milling percentage : 60%
■Acid degree: 1.4
■Sake meter value: −1
■Recommended retail price:
 189 yen（150 ml）,
 420 yen（300 ml）,
 997 yen（720 ml）,
 2,100 yen（1800 ml）
■Type of taste: Slightly sweet

福光屋（石川）

そのはじまりは江戸時代にさかのぼる、金沢で最も長い歴史と伝統を誇る酒蔵。「伝統は革新の連続」の言葉通り、職人魂の酒造りを貫きながら、時代ごとの変化を遂げている。現在では、「マルチブランド」政策のもと、それぞれのブランドに、明確なターゲット、およびターゲットシーン、全く独立したコンセプトを持ち、酒の造りも、その味わいも全く異なる。純米酒のみで造る。また、地元金沢や東京・銀座には福光屋の酒や酒器だけでなく、米発酵をキーワードとした多彩な商品を提案するショップを経営。サケスクールも人気。

Fukumitsuya（Ishikawa Prefecture）
Established in the Edo period（1603-1867）. Boasts longest history and tradition in Kanazawa, an old city facing the Japan Sea. While maintaining craftsmanship, responds to changes of the times. Seeks multi-brand policies. Produces junmai-shu only. Operates junmai-shu and sake cup & container shops in Kanazawa and Ginza, Tokyo.

福正宗 氷温生貯蔵酒

自然の旨さとさらっとした後味が特長の福正宗はハウスブランド。会話を引き立て、楽しいコミュニケーションを創造していく日常の酒、が福正宗のコンセプト。この氷温生貯蔵酒は厳寒の酒蔵で仕込んだ純米酒をそのまま氷温で貯蔵したもの。しぼりたてのドライな旨さが特長。

- アルコール度数：13度以上14度未満
- 原材料：米・米こうじ
- 精米歩合：65.0%
- 酸度：1.50
- 日本酒度：＋10.0
- 希望小売価格：316円（180ml）、438円（300ml）
- 味のタイプ：辛口

Fukumasamune Raw Sake Stored Below Freezing
Light aftertaste. In-house brand. The concept of this o-sake is to contribute to better communication at casual dining tables. Stored at below the freezing point. Dry taste is distinctive.

- Alcohol: From 13% to less than 14%
- Ingredients: Rice and malted rice
- Rice milling percentage: 65.0%
- Acid degree: 1.50
- Sake meter value: +10.0
- Recommended retail price: 316 yen (180 ml), 438 yen (300 ml)
- Type of taste: Dry

株式会社福光屋　石川県金沢市石引2-8-3
Tel. 076-223-1161　http://www.fukumitsuya.co.jp
Fukumitsuya Sake Brewery　2-8-3, Ishibiki, Kanazawa City, Ishikawa Prefecture

---

武重（長野）

創業は明治元年。武重本家酒造と武重家の30の建造物が国の登録有形文化財に指定されている、歴史と風格ある蔵元。「生酛造り」をかたくなに守り続け、「御園竹」に代表されるような地元で愛される酒を造り続ける一方で、時代の先を読む新しい酒の開発にも力を入れる、まさに温故知新の酒造りをする。毎年1回、春分の日は「酒蔵開放」の日で、酒造蔵の見学のほか、ケーキやソーセージなどといった、さまざまな食べ物と日本酒の相性を提案するなどの試みをしている。

Takeshige（Nagano Prefecture）
Established in 1868. Thirty buildings of the Takeshige Honke Brewing Corp. and the Takeshige family's homes have been designated as important cultural properties by the Japanese government. In addition to making *jizake*, or rural o-sake, it also produces o-sake that sets the trend of the new era. Each year on Spring Equinox Day (a national holiday in Japan) they open their storerooms to the public. They are rediscovering o-sake in the traditional context of Japanese-style cuisine and also as a liquor that can be enjoyed on any occasion.

やんわり（純米酒）

疲れた身体にやさしい極めて甘口のお酒です。思い切り冷やすとおいしい、酸味が抑えられた低アルコール酒。食後のゆったりとした時間にディジェスティフとして楽しむのにも向いた味わい。

- アルコール度数：11度
- 原材料：米・米こうじ
- 精米歩合：58%
- 酸度：2.3
- 日本酒度：－41
- 希望小売価格：473円（300ml）
- 味のタイプ：甘口

Yanwari
Extremely sweet. This o-sake has a healing effect. Best chilled. Subdued acidity and low alcohol. Good as a digestif.

- Alcohol: 11%
- Ingredients: Rice and malted rice
- Rice milling percentage: 58%
- Acid degree: 2.3
- Sake meter value: −41
- Recommended retail price: 473 yen (300 ml)
- Type of taste: Sweet

武重本家酒造株式会社　長野県北佐久郡望月町茂田井2179
Tel.0267-53-3025　http://www.takeshige-honke.co.jp/
Takeshige-honke Brewing Corp.　2179, Motai, Mochizuki-machi, Kitasaku-gun, Nagano Prefecture.

小山酒造（東京）

東京 Tokyo

創業は明治11年。東京都北区岩淵町にあり、23区に残る蔵元としてはオンリーワン。秩父山系、浦和水脈の伏流水を地下130メートルから汲み上げ、その地下水（硬水）を原水に、自家栽培酵母で醸造する酒は、「東京の地酒」「江戸の地酒」として、全国的に幅広い支持を受けている。蔵見学の希望者が年々増え続けているという蔵元。

Koyama Shuzou (Tokyo)

Established in 1878. Located in Iwabuchi-cho, Kita-ku. Made using hard water, or local ground water in the outskirts of Tokyo. O-sake produced by this brewer are well received as *jizake* or local sake of Tokyo. Increasing number of sightseers visit yearly.

丸眞正宗 吟の舞（純米大吟醸酒）

香り高く、ソフトな味わい。1986年と1993年の東京サミットの晩餐会では、レセプション時の乾杯酒"Japanese Sake"として各国首脳に饗され、好評を得た国際派の日本酒。東京、千葉、神奈川、山梨の蔵元数十社による銘酒開発協同組合の共同銘柄推奨酒のひとつ。

- ■アルコール度数:13.4度 ■原材料:米・米こうじ ■精米歩合:50% ■酸度:1.5
- ■日本酒度:2.0 ■希望小売価格:2,243円(720ml) ■味のタイプ:やや辛口

Marushin Masamune Gin no Mai

A savory bouquet and soft palate (Dai-ginjo Junmai-shu). Served at the banquets during the Tokyo G-7 Summit Meetings in 1986 and 1993 and well received. An o-sake of international caliber. Jointly developed by several brewers.

- ■Alcohol: 13.4%
- ■Ingredients: Rice and malted rice
- ■Rice milling percentage: 50%
- ■Acid degree: 1.5
- ■Sake meter value: +2
- ■Recommended retail price: 2,243 yen (720 ml),
- ■Type of taste: sligtly dry

小山酒造株式会社　東京都北区岩淵町26-10
Tel.03-3902-3451　http://www.kitanet.ne.jp/~m-koyama/kaisya.ht
Koyama Shuzou　26-10, Iwabuchi-cho, Kita-ku, Tokyo

井上酒造（神奈川）

神奈川 Kanagawa

寛政元年（1789）創業、神奈川県内でも老舗の酒蔵。代表銘柄の「箱根山」は、約30年前、ヨーロッパ諸国に輸出をはじめるにあたり、海外でも通用する銘柄を検討した結果、会社のある敷地から毎日眺めることが出来、日本を代表し世界的な観光地でもある箱根にちなんで名付けられた。現在も、海外へ輸出されている。

Inouyc Brewing (Kanagawa Prefecture)

Established in 1789. One of the oldest brewers in the prefecture. Renowned for Hakoneyama brand. Named after the famous resort in the prefecture, Hakone, in 1970s. Commands a nice view. Has been exported since then overseas.

スイートハート（純米酒）

アルコール度5%のスパークリング酒。瓶内に封じ込まれた炭酸ガスのシュワッとした爽快感と甘酸っぱい味わいが特徴。おめでたい席での乾杯用のお酒として、また日本酒の苦手な方や弱い方におすすめ。

- ■アルコール度数:4.5度以上5.5未満 ■原材料:米・米こうじ ■精米歩合:70%
- ■酸度:3.7 ■日本酒度:ー80 ■希望小売価格:630円(300ml) ■味のタイプ:甘口

"Sweet Heart"

Sparkling junmai-shu, 5% alcohol. Carbon dioxide gas in the bottle gives a refreshing palate. Sweet and sour taste. Suitable for auspicious occasions. Recommended to occasional sake drinkers.

- ■Alcohol: From 4.5% to less than 5.5%
- ■Ingredients: Rice and rice malt
- ■Rice milling percentage: 70%
- ■Acid degree: 3.7
- ■Sake meter value: −80
- ■Recommended retail price: 630 yen (300 ml)
- ■Type of taste: Sweet

井上酒造株式会社　神奈川県足柄上郡大井町上大井552
Tel.0465-82-0325
INOUYE BREWING CO., LTD.　552, Kami-oi, Oi-machi, Ashigara Kami-gun, Kanagawa Prefecture

宝酒造（京都）

業界のリーディングカンパニーは、2001年に灘工場を一新させ、伝統的な手造りの原理を再現し、最新の設備を備える「松竹梅白壁蔵」として生まれ変わった。飲んだ瞬間にその酒を造った人たちの顔、その酒が生まれた蔵の姿を想いめぐらすことの出来るような酒を造ることを目標に、次世代の蔵人育成にも力を入れる。また「お米とお酒の学校」なども開設し、食育やエコロジー活動にも積極的に取り組んでいる。

Takara Shuzo (Kyoto)
A leading brewer in Japan. Renovated its factory in Nada, Kobe Prefecture, with state of the art technology. Keen on ecology and educating brewers for the next generation; opening a school to teach about rice and sake.

宝酒造株式会社
京都府京都市伏見区竹中町
609番地
Tel.075-241-5111
http://www.takarashuzo.co.jp
Takara Shuzo Co., Ltd.
609, Takenaka-cho,
Fushimi-ku, Kyoto

上撰松竹梅 超淡麗辛口「生冷酒」焙炒造り

宝酒造独自の特許製法である「焙炒造り」による、超淡麗辛口の清酒。掛米を蒸さず、熱風で瞬間的に処理するので、アミノ酸や脂肪量が通常の日本酒よりも少なく、すっきりとした味わいで飲みやすくなる。冷やすことで、よりサラリと味わえる。

■アルコール度数：14度以上15度未満　■原材料：米・米こうじ・醸造アルコール　■精米歩合：ー　■酸度：1.1　■日本酒度：+10.0　■希望小売価格：234円(180ml)、372円(300ml)　■味のタイプ：辛口

**Josen Sho-chiku-bai
Chou Tanrei Karakuchi
"Raw cold sake" Roasting Method**
Brewed with its proprietary roasting method. Highly refreshing. Best chilled.
■Alcohol: From 14% to less than 15%
■Ingredients: Rice, malted rice, and brewer's alcohol
■Rice milling percentage: ー
■Acid degree: 1.1
■Sake meter value: +10.0
■Recommended retail price: 234 yen (180 ml), 372 yen (300 ml)
■Type of taste: Dry

上撰 松竹梅「たけ」

「竹」をかたどったパッケージで親しみのある酒。蓋を取るとそのままぐい飲みになり、アウトドアなどのレジャーに便利な作りになっている。

■アルコール度数：15度以上16度未満　■原材料：米・米こうじ・醸造アルコール　■酸度：1.3　■日本酒度：+1　■希望小売価格：225円(180ml)、372円(300ml)　■味のタイプ：辛口

Josen Sho-chiku-bai "Take (Bamboo)"
Bamboo shaped package. The lid of the bottle of this o-sake can be used as a cup. Convenient for outdoor leisure use.
■Alcohol: From 15% to less than 16%
■Ingredients: Rice, malted rice, and brewer's alcohol
■Rice milling percentage: ー
■Acid degree: 1.3
■Sake meter value: +1
■Recommended retail price: 225 yen (180 ml), 372 yen (300 ml)
■Type of taste: Dry

松竹梅白壁蔵「三谷藤夫」〈山廃純米〉〈純米酒〉

「三谷藤夫」は杜氏の名。経験と磨きぬかれた五感を備えた杜氏三谷氏が、「松竹梅白壁蔵」で造る、こだわりの名酒。純米酒らしい豊かな風味を持ちつつ、山廃ならではの芳醇で深い味わいがある。喉越しもよく、飲み飽きのこない、すべてにバランスのとれた酒。

■アルコール度数：15度以上16度未満　■原材料：米・米こうじ　■精米歩合：60%　■酸度：1.5　■日本酒度：+2　■希望小売価格：1,260円(720ml)、2,520円(1800ml)　■味のタイプ：辛口

Sho-chiku-bai Shirakabegura "Mitani Fujio" Yamahai Junmai
Named after a touji, Fujjio Mitani. Profound taste and characteristic bouquet made under the Yamahai method. Goes down smoothly and does not cloy the palate. Well-balanced.
■Alcohol: From 15% to less than 16%
■Ingredients: Rice and malted rice
■Rice milling percentage: 60%
■Acid degree: 1.5
■Sake meter value: +2
■Recommended retail price: 1,260 yen (720 ml), 2,520 yen (1800 ml)
■Type of taste: Dry

山縣（山口）

創業明治8年の、瀬戸内の歴史ある蔵元。「毛利公」に代表される伝統を守りつつ、酒蔵でじっくり寝かせた米焼酎、地元周南市産の梅を使った梅酒、夏みかんのリキュール造りなど、絶えず新しい試みにも挑戦している。原材料の品質には特にこだわり、夏みかんは、萩市堀内の農園で栽培された無農薬のものを使用。

Yamagata Honten (Yamaguchi Prefecture)
Established in 1875. Close to Kyushu and facing the Seto Inland Sea. Famous for its traditional o-sake, Mouri-kou. They use choice plums grown in Shunan City and chemical-free summer oranges from Hagi City, Yamaguchi Prefecture.

山口 Yamaguchi

株式会社山縣本店
山口県周南市久米2933
Tel.0834-25-0048
http://www.oboshi.co.jp/kuramoto/yamagata/
Yamagata Honten Co.,Ltd.
2933, Kume, Shunan City, Yamaguchi Prefecture.

純米大吟醸 毛利公（純米大吟醸酒）

山縣本店の代表銘柄。「最後の熊毛杜氏（山口県熊毛出身の杜氏）」と言われている中坪忠夫氏の手による特別な大吟醸酒。こうじ作りから全て人の手を使い膨大な労力を重ねてつくられている。その香り高さは、通常の2倍の時間をかけ低温発酵させたことによる。

■アルコール度数:16.5度　■原材料:米・米こうじ　■精米歩合:35%　■酸度:1.4　■日本酒度:+4.5　■希望小売価格:3,675円(720ml)　■味のタイプ:やや甘口

Junmai Dai-ginjo Mouri-kou
Produces many kinds of sake under different brand names, but Mouri-kou is the most popular one.
Made by the last touji, master sake brewer, in this district. Made by hand mainly. Fermented under low temperature. Accordingly, it is fragrant.

- Alcohol: 16.5 %
- Ingredients: Rice and malted rice
- Rice milling percentage: 35%
- Acid degree: 1.4
- Sake meter value: +4.5
- Recommended retail price: 3,675 yen (720 ml)
- Type of taste: Slightly sweet

花かほり（純米吟醸酒）

桜の花から造られた「やまぐち・桜酵母」を使用した、低アルコールタイプの日本酒。酵母が放つ、甘味とフルーティーな香りが特徴で、「かほり」と命名された。ふんわりとやわらかな味わいが、春の花畑を連想させる。国内のみならず、欧米にも出荷され、人気を博している。

■アルコール度数:13.5度　■原材料:米・米こうじ　■精米歩合:50%　■酸度:1.3　■日本酒度:+1.0　■希望小売価格:525円(300ml)　■味のタイプ:やや甘口

Hana no Kaori
Low alcohol. Made with cherry blossom yeast. Named after its distinctive sweet and fruity bouquet. Well-received at home and abroad. The luscious taste reminds me of a flower garden in spring.

- Alcohol:13.5%
- Ingredients: Rice and malted rice
- Rice milling percentage: 50%
- Acid degree: 1.3
- Sake meter value: +1.0
- Recommended retail price: 525 yen (300 ml)
- Type of taste: Slightly sweet

本醸造かほり鶴 昔づくり（本醸造酒）

本醸造といえば、今では醸造用アルコールを添加することが一般的だが、このお酒は江戸中期の文献をもとに、酒粕より蒸留した焼酎を添加する「柱焼酎」という手法で造られたこだわりの味。5年間熟成させた焼酎を添加したお酒の味わいは、キリッと粋な江戸の味。

■アルコール度数:14.5度　■原材料:米・米こうじ・本格焼酎　■精米歩合:70%　■酸度:1.7　■日本酒度:+4.0　■希望小売価格:917円(720ml)　■味のタイプ:やや辛口

Honjo-zo Kaori Duru Mukashi Dukuri
Made with sake lees and distilled spirit, according to the method conducted in mid 18th century. The mellowed spirit is five years old. Crisp taste.

- Alcohol: 14.5 %
- Ingredients: Rice, malted rice, and rice spirit.
- Rice milling percentage: 70%
- Acid degree: 1.7
- Sake meter value: +4.0
- Recommended retail price: 917 yen (720 ml)
- Type of taste: Slightly dry

本書に表示されている価格は、消費税を含んでいます。
＊The prices in this book include consumption tax levied in Japan.

『Osakeでスイーツ』に登場した特定名称酒 Types of Sake in "Sake with Desserts"

[特定名称の清酒の表示について]
吟醸酒、純米酒、本醸造酒を特定名称の清酒といい、原料、製造方法の違いによって8種類に分類されます。
それぞれ所定の要件に該当するものにその名称を表示することが出来ます。

Japanese sake is classified into three basic types: Junmai-shu (pure rice sake), honjo-zo [honjo-dukuri] (no glucose and less raw alcohol added during brewing process), and ginjo-shu (special type of junmai-shu or honjo-zo). These come under the refined sake category. These three types are classified into eight categories according to ingredients and brewing process. If a sake falls into one of the eight categories, the sake brewer can print the name of the category on the label.

特定名称 Types of Sake	使用原料 Ingredients	精米歩合 Rice Milling Percentage	こうじ米の使用割合 Rate of Rice Malt Used	香味等の要件 Flavor Requirement, etc.
吟醸酒 Ginjo-shu	米、米こうじ、醸造アルコール Rice, malted rice, and brewer's alcohol	60％以下 60% or less than 60%	15％以上 15% or more than 15%	吟醸造り 固有の香味、色沢が良好 Ginjo brewing method Distinctive flavor and good clarity
大吟醸酒 Dai-ginjo-shu (Grand ginjo-shu)	米、米こうじ、醸造アルコール Rice, malted rice, and brewer's alcohol	50％以下 50% or less than 50%	15％以上 15% or more than 15%	吟醸造り 固有の香味、色沢が特に良好 Ginjo brewing method Distinctive flavor and pristine clarity
純米酒 Junmai-shu	米、米こうじ Rice and malted rice	―	15％以上 15% or more than 15%	香味、色沢が良好 Flavor and good clarity
純米吟醸酒 Junmai ginjo-shu	米、米こうじ Rice and malted rice	60％以下 60% or less than 60%	15％以上 15% or more than 15%	吟醸造り 固有の香味、色沢が良好 Ginjo brewing method Distinctive flavor and good clarity
純米大吟醸酒 Junmai dai-ginjo-shu	米、米こうじ Rice and malted rice	50％以下 50% or less than 50%	15％以上 15% or more than 15%	吟醸造り 固有の香味、色沢が特に良好 Ginjo brewing method Distinctive flavor and pristine clarity
特別純米酒 Tokubetsu junmai-shu (Special junmai-shu)	米、米こうじ Rice and malted rice	60％以下、または特別な製造方法（要説明表示） 60% or less than 60% Or special brewing process	15％以上 15% or more than 15%	香味、色沢が特に良好 Flavor and pristine clarity
本醸造酒 Honjo-zo-shu	米、米こうじ、醸造アルコール Rice, malted rice, and brewer's alcohol	70％以下 70% or less than 70%	15％以上 15% or more than 15%	香味、色沢が良好 Flavor and good clarity
特別本醸造酒 Tokubetsu-honjo-zo-shu	米、米こうじ、醸造アルコール Rice, malted rice, and brewer's alcohol	60％以下、または特別な製造方法（要説明表示） 60% or less than 60% Or special brewing process	15％以上 15% or more than 15%	香味、色沢が特に良好 Flavor and pristine clarity

● 参考資料／国税庁「清酒の製法品質表示基準」より
● Source: "Standard for labels describing the method for producing sake" prescribed by the National Tax Administration Agency in Japan.

おわりに

「お酒、かなりいけそうですね」。最近、仕事先でこう言われることが多くなり、喜んでいいのやら返答に悩みます。

今や、日本だけに限らず、欧米各国における世界的な健康志向の高まりによって、アルコール飲料を含めた食事に関する考え方は、量より質が重視される時代になりました。けれども残念なことに、その質とは、食品の安全性や栄養学的視点からみた健康面に関することがほとんどです。誰と一緒に、どんな風に食べるのかといった、食事をする場面の環境の質については、あまり触れられていないようです。

しかし、栄養学的に、どんなに優れた食事をしていても、それだけでは健康になれないように、食べたり、飲んだりする場面には、人とのコミュニケーションが欠かせません。そして、そのコミュニケーションの場のしつらえは、食卓を囲んでいる人たちひとりひとりの心に、大きな影響を与えます。健康な心身は、そうした食事をする環境の質も考えた「楽しい食卓」がもたらしてくれると信じている私は、「Osake、かなり楽しくいけるほう」だと思います。

この本を読んで下さった皆さんが、「さて、それでは一杯のOsakeをどんな風に楽しんでみようか」と思いめぐらされたとしたら、こんなにうれしいことはありません。

最後になりましたが、この本を出版するにあたり心よくお引き受けいただいたギャップ・ジャパンの梁田義秋(やなだよしあき)社長をはじめ、お力添えをいただきました多くの皆様方に、心から感謝申し上げます。ありがとうございました。

Epilogue

Nowadays, an increasing number of people pay more attention to healthy diet, and put more importance on quality from the perspective of nutritional science, not on the perspective of the ambience of dining.

Nutritional balance alone does not make people healthy. Good conversation and pleasing table settings provide an appetizing background for meals. I believe such an atmosphere contributes to our well-being.

Therefore, I would like to provide a new dimension in table setting design to enhance the overall experience.

I would be pleased if readers of this book enjoy creating a fresh individual look for their dining table.

I would like to take this opportunity to extend my sincere appreciation to Mr. Yoshiaki Yanada, Chairperson of Gap Japan Co., Ltd. for kindly accepting my book proposal and to all the people concerned with the various aspects of this book for their kind assistance.

Index

(順不同)

■ メーカー問い合わせ先一覧

● スイーツ

① シーキューブ 丸ビル店	☎ 03-5220-7055
② エモーションズ	☎ 03-3414-8555
③ 京橋千疋屋 表参道原宿店	☎ 03-3403-2550
④ 日本アンカー	☎ 03-3501-1311
⑤ 北見ハッカ通商	☎ 0157-66-5655
⑥ 木風(玉川高島屋SC本館B1F フーズシティ)	☎ 03-3709-0002
⑦ ベルン	📞 0120-048-371
⑧ 京とうふ藤野	☎ 075-463-1035
⑨ モロゾフお客様サービスセンター	☎ 078-822-5533
⑩ ユーハイム	📞 0120-860816
⑪ パティシエ イナムラ ショウゾウ	☎ 03-3827-8584
⑫ 菓匠 叶 匠壽庵	☎ 077-546-5300
⑬ ふらんす菓子クローバー	📞 0120-89-9681
⑭ キル フェ ボン	☎ 03-5414-7741
⑮ オーボンヴュータン	☎ 03-3703-8428
⑯ ラトリエ ドゥ ジョエル・ロブション	☎ 03-5772-7507
⑰ スイートランド・ナチュラルスイーツ	☎ 03-3535-6856
⑱ 山縣本店	☎ 0834-25-0048
⑲ 浪花屋製菓	☎ 0258-23-2201
⑳ 松月堂	📞 0120-08-3008
㉑ とらや	📞 0120-45-4121
㉒ 神戸、元町 一番舘	☎ 078-391-3138
㉓ シリアルマミー	📞 0120-89-5904
㉔ ル ショコラ ドゥ アッシュ	☎ 03-5772-0075

● 器

Ⓐ 日本の酒情報館 SAKE PLAZA	☎ 03-3519-2091
Ⓑ Sugahara	☎ 03-5468-8131
Ⓒ 玉有	☎ 0955-43-2384
Ⓓ 漆楽 URUSHIRAKU	☎ 03-3362-7651
Ⓔ 大阪錫器	☎ 06-6628-6731
Ⓕ 玉川堂	☎ 0256-62-2015
Ⓖ 東京カットグラス工業協同組合	☎ 03-3681-0961
Ⓗ ちきりや	☎ 0264-34-2002
Ⓘ HOYA(株)クリスタルカンパニー	📞 0120-556-711
Ⓙ 船崎窯	☎ 0838-25-5154
Ⓚ ジアン青山本店	☎ 03-3470-0613
Ⓛ 洸春陶苑	☎ 075-561-5388
Ⓜ 栗久	☎ 0186-42-0514
Ⓝ 象彦	☎ 075-752-7777
Ⓞ 日樽	☎ 0186-48-4153
Ⓟ カネコ小兵製陶所	☎ 0572-57-8168
Ⓠ リーデル・ジャパン	☎ 03-5775-5888
Ⓡ リーン・ロゼ青山	☎ 03-5771-5800
Ⓢ ニッコー	☎ 076-276-2121
Ⓣ 河田	☎ 03-3209-8351

● リネン

| Ⓤ ケイズ・コンポジション | ☎ 042-522-3547 |

■ For inquiries about for the products in this book:

● Desserts

① C³	☎ 03-5220-7055
② Favorite Co., Ltd.	☎ 03-3414-8555
③ Kyobashi Senbikiya, Omotesando Harajuku Branch	☎ 03-3403-2550
④ Anchor Japan Co., Ltd.	☎ 03-3501-1311
⑤ Kitami Hakka Tsusho Co., Ltd.	☎ 0157-66-5655
⑥ KIKAZE. Foods City B1F Tamagawa Takashimaya S.C	☎ 03-3709-0002
⑦ Berne Co., Ltd.	📞 0120-048-371
⑧ Kyotofu Fujino	☎ 075-463-1035
⑨ Morozoff	☎ 078-822-5533
⑩ Juchheim Co., Ltd.	📞 0120-860816
⑪ PÂTISSIER INAMURA SHOZO	☎ 03-3827-8584
⑫ KANO SHOJUAN	☎ 077-546-5300
⑬ PÂTISSERIE CLOVER	📞 0120-89-9681
⑭ Qu'il Fait Bon	☎ 03-5414-7741
⑮ Au Bon Vieux Temps	☎ 03-3703-8428
⑯ L'ATELIER de Joël Robuchon	☎ 03-5772-7507
⑰ Sweetland Co., Ltd.	☎ 03-3535-6856
⑱ Yamagata Honten Co., Ltd.	☎ 0834-25-0048
⑲ NANIWAYASEIKA CO., LTD.	☎ 0258-23-2201
⑳ Shogetsudo Co., Ltd.	📞 0120-08-3008
㉑ TORAYA	📞 0120-45-4121
㉒ Ichibankàn Co., Ltd.	☎ 078-391-3138
㉓ cereal mammy	📞 0120-89-5904
㉔ LE CHOCOLAT DE H	☎ 03-5772-0075

● Serving dish

Ⓐ SAKE PLAZA	☎ 03-3519-2091
Ⓑ SUGAHARA GLASSWORKS INC.	☎ 03-5468-8131
Ⓒ Gyokuyu	☎ 0955-43-2384
Ⓓ Urushiraku	☎ 03-3362-7651
Ⓔ Osaka Suzuki Co., Ltd.	☎ 06-6628-6731
Ⓕ GYOKUSENDO CO., LTD.	☎ 0256-62-2015
Ⓖ Cooperative Association of Tokyo Cut Glass Kogyo	☎ 03-3681-0961
Ⓗ Chikiriya Inc.	☎ 0264-34-2002
Ⓘ HOYA CORPORATION Crystal Company	📞 0120-556-711
Ⓙ Funasaki-gama	☎ 0838-25-5154
Ⓚ Gien Aoyama Boutique	☎ 03-3470-0613
Ⓛ Kousyun Touen	☎ 075-561-5388
Ⓜ Kurikyu	☎ 0186-42-0514
Ⓝ ZOHIKO CORPORATION	☎ 075-752-7777
Ⓞ Nittaru Ltd.	☎ 0186-48-4153
Ⓟ KANEKO KO-HYO POTTERY MANUFACTURING CO., LTD.	☎ 0572-57-8168
Ⓠ RIEDEL JAPAN CO., LTD.	☎ 03-5775-5888
Ⓡ ligne roset aoyama	☎ 03-5771-5800
Ⓢ NIKKO COMPANY	☎ 076-276-2121
Ⓣ KAWADA CO., LTD.	☎ 03-3209-8351

● Linen

| Ⓤ LE JACQUARD FRANÇAIS | ☎ 042-522-3547 |

103

Osakeでスイーツ

2004年 6月 20日　初版第一刷発行

著者	：手島麻記子
発行者	：梁田義秋
発行元	：株式会社ギャップ・ジャパン.
発売元	：株式会社ジャパン・プランニング・アソシエーション
	〒150-0011 東京都渋谷区東3-9-12
販売部	：TEL　03-5778-7170
	FAX　03-5766-6401
印刷製本	：三松堂印刷株式会社

ブックデザイン	：小熊千佳子（MOVE Art Management）
撮影	：中川 彰　（MOVE Art Management）
スタイリング	：手島麻記子（彩食絢美）
編集	：山形尚孝　（ギャップ・ジャパン）
	松原正世　（strange days）
翻訳	：金子 恵
英文編集	：アラン・マーフィー

Special thanks
彩食絢美・五十嵐裕美子・松澤裕子・山上珠紀の各氏、彩食絢美の卒業生・在校生の皆さん。冨永眞哉、中山加奈子（日本外国特派員協会図書室）、Alex Routh、William Fedchuk、高崎綾子、およびカメラマン・アシスタント・黒瀬ゆかりの各氏。

定価はカバーに表示してあります。乱丁・落丁がありましたときはお取り替え致します。
本書の無断転載・複写（コピー）は、著作権上の例外を除き、禁じられております。
©Makiko Tejima　Printed in Japan　ISBN4-88357-209-9

Sake with Desserts

First published on June 20, 2004

Author	: Makiko Tejima
Chairperson	: Yoshiaki Yanada
Publisher	: Gap Japan Co., Ltd.
Selling Agency	: Japan Planning Association Co., Ltd.
Address of Publisher	: 3-9-12, Higashi Shibuya-ku, Tokyo 150-0011
Sales Department	: TEL 03-5778-7170
	FAX 03-5766-6401
Printing and Binding	: SANSHODO. PRINTING CO., LTD.

Book Designer	: Chikako Oguma（MOVE Art Management）
Photographer	: Akira Nakagawa（MOVE Art Management）
Decorator	: Makiko Tejima　（Sai-Shoku-Ken-Bi）
Editor	: Hisanori Yamagata（GAP JAPAN）
	Masayo Matsubara（Strange Days）
Translator	: Megumi Kaneko
Editor(English)	: Allan Murphy

Special thanks
Makiko Tejima: Ms. Yumiko Igarashi, Ms. Yuko Matsuzawa, Ms. Tamaki Yamagami and the graduates and students of Sai-Shoku-Ken-Bi.
Megumi Kaneko: Mr. Shinya Tominaga, Mrs. Kanako Nakayama (FCCJ), Mr. Alex Routh, Mr. William Fedchuk, and Ms. Ayako Takasaki.
And thanks to Ms. Yukari Kurose, the assistant photographer and to everyone concerned with this book.

The price of this book is printed on the cover. In case there is a missing page or erratic pagination, you will receive a replacement. No part of this book may be used or reproduced in any manner whatsoever without written permission except in the case of brief quotations embodied in articles and reviews.

SAKE WITH DESSERTS: Copyright © 2004 by MakikoTejima
All rights reserved.
Printed in Japan
First edition, 2004
ISBN4-88357-209-9